GREATEST HITS

the 1960s FOR PIANO

Over 40 Pop Music Favorites

Woodstock
JONI MITCHELL

Hair
THE COWSILLS

You Showed Me
THE TURTLES

James Bond Theme
THE MONTY NORMAN ORCHESTRA

96 Tears
? AND THE MYSTERIANS

A Summer Song
CHAD & JEREMY

Kind of a Drag
THE BUCKINGHAMS

What's New Pussycat?
TOM JONES

Aquarius/Let the Sunshine In
THE 5TH DIMENSION

You Don't Have to Say You Love Me
DUSTY SPRINGFIELD

(I Can't Get No) Satisfaction
THE ROLLING STONES

Put a Little Love in Your Heart
JACKIE DeSHANNON

A Taste of Honey
HERB ALPERT & THE TIJUANA BRASS

Goldfinger
SHIRLEY BASSEY

Do You Want to Know a Secret
THE BEATLES

Time of the Season
THE ZOMBIES

Leaving on a Jet Plane
PETER, PAUL & MARY

Pinball Wizard
THE WHO

Eight Miles High
THE BYRDS

Mustang Sally
WILSON PICKETT

Lay Lady Lay
BOB DYLAN

Produced by
Alfred Music
P.O. Box 10003
Van Nuys, CA 91410-0003
alfred.com

Printed in USA.

ISBN-10: 1-4706-1702-1
ISBN-13: 978-1-4706-1702-8

Artist Index

Contents

96 TEARS

Words and Music by
RUDY MARTINEZ

Moderate surf beat ♩ = 120

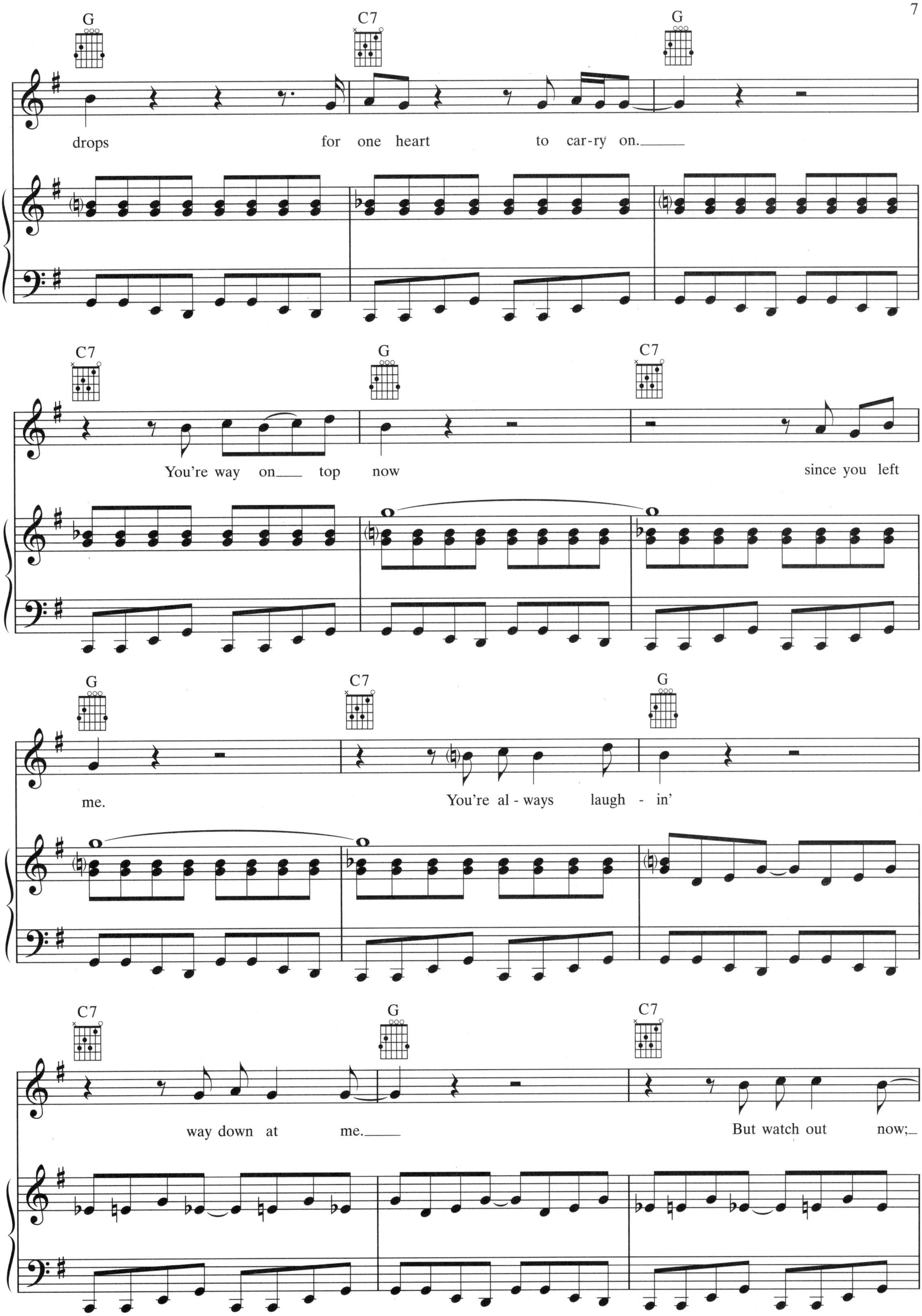
G
C7
G
drops for one heart to car-ry on.
C7
G
C7
You're way on top now since you left
G
C7
G
me. You're al-ways laugh-in'
C7
G
C7
way down at me. But watch out now;

G
C7
G
I'm gon - na get there.
C7
G
C7
We'll be to - geth - er
for just a lit - tle while.
G
C7
G
And then I'm gon - na put you
C7
G
C7
way down here.
And you'll start cry -

G
C7
G
in'
nine - ty - six tears.
C7
G
C7
Cry,
cry.
Bridge:
G
C7
Em
And when the sun comes up,
I'll be on top.
You'll be right down there
look - in' up.

And I might wave,
"Come up here."
But I don't_ see you_
wav-in' now.
I'm way down here
won-d'rin' how
I'm gon-na get you.
But I know now
C
G
C7
I'll just cry,
cry,___
I'll just cry.

G
C7
Too man-y tear - drops
for one heart
G
C7
G
to be cry - in'.
Too man-y tear - drops
for
C7
G
C7
one heart
to car - ry on.
You're gon - na
Chorus:
G
C7
G
cry
nine - ty - six tears.
You're gon - na
cry
nine - ty - six tears.

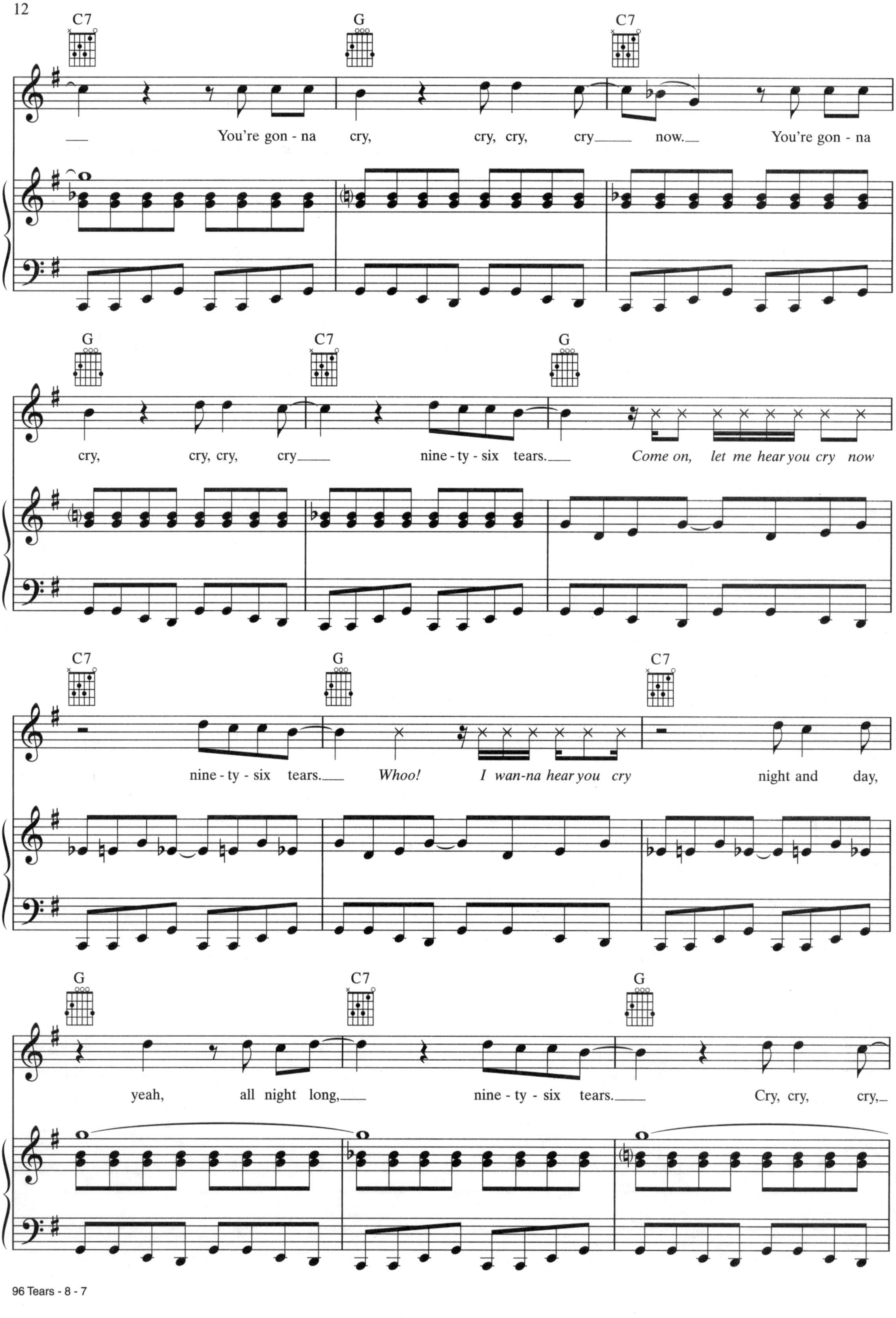
C7 G C7
You're gon - na cry, cry, cry, cry now. You're gon - na
G C7 G
cry, cry, cry, cry nine - ty - six tears. Come on, let me hear you cry now
C7 G C7
nine - ty - six tears. Whoo! I wan-na hear you cry night and day,
G C7 G
yeah, all night long, nine - ty - six tears. Cry, cry, cry,

C7
G
C7
come on, ba - by, let me hear you cry now, all night long, a - nine - ty - six tears.
G
C7
G
Yeah! Come on now, a - nine - ty - six tears.
Repeat and fade
C7
G
C7

AQUARIUS/LET THE SUNSHINE IN

Lyrics by
JAMES RADO and
GEROME RAGNI

Music by
GALT MacDERMOT

Bright rock ♩ = 183

Cm9 F7/C Cm9
peace will guide the plan - ets and
E♭ F7 B♭ N.C.
love will steer the stars. This is the dawn - ing of the
cresc. poco a poco
Chorus:
A♭
age of A - quar - i - us, age of A - quar - i - us.
mf
Cm F
A - quar - i - us.
cresc. poco a poco

Cm
A - quar - i - us.
To Coda
Bridge:
B♭7
E♭
Har - mo - ny and un - der - stand - ing,
f
B♭7
E♭
B♭7
sym - pa - thy and trust a - bound - ing.
No more false-hoods or de - ri -
E♭
Cm
G7/D
E♭
G7/D
sions, gold - en liv - ing dreams of vi-sions, mys - tic crys - tal rev - e - la -

Cm
Cm7
Fm
Gm
tion, and the mind's true lib - er - a - tion. A -
Fm
quar - i - us. A -
Cm
quar - i - us.
p
Cm9
Cm
Cm9
Cm
D.S. 𝄋 al Coda
N.C.
When the
mp

Coda
F
A - quar - i - us.
Cm
A - quar - i - us.
Moderate rock ♩ = 120
Bm
F♯7
f
Bm
G
D

Bm
F#7
Let the sun - shine.
Let the sun -
f–ff
Bm
G
D
shine in, the sun - shine in.
Bm
F#7
Let the sun - shine.
Let the sun -
Bm
G
D
Repeat and fade
shine in, the sun - shine in.

BECAUSE

Words and Music by
DAVE CLARK

D
D+
hap - py when you're blue.
It's
G
G+
C
right, it's right to feel the way I
Cm
G
Am
D7
do be - cause, be - cause I love
Bridge:
G
Am
you.
It's wrong to

D
G
Em
say I don't think of you.
Am
D7
A
'Cause when you say these things, you know it makes me blue.
Verse 2:
D7
D+
G
G+
2. Give me one kiss and I'll be
G6
G7
Am
hap - py, just,

D
D+
just to be with you.
Give
G
G+
C
me, give me a chance to be
Cm
G
Am
D7
near you be - cause, be - cause I love
G
E♭
D
G
G+
you.

G6
G7
Am
D
D7
G
E♭
D
Verse 3:
G
3. Give me one
G+
G6
G7
kiss and I'll be hap - py,
Am
D
just, just to be with you.

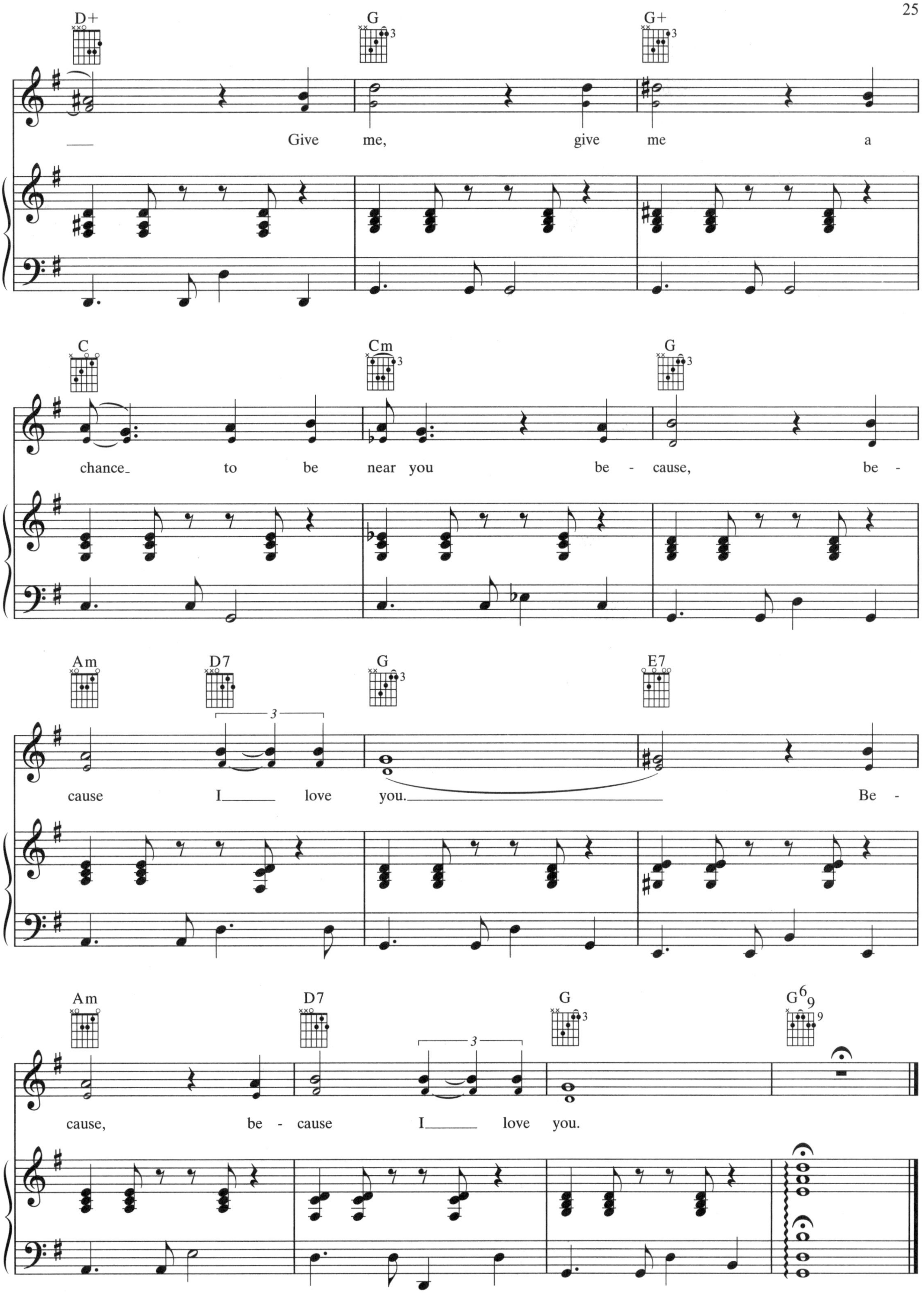
D+ G G+
Give me, give me a
C Cm G
chance to be near you be - cause, be -
Am D7 G E7
cause I love you. Be -
Am D7 G G6/9
cause, be - cause I love you.

BUILD ME UP BUTTERCUP

Words and Music by
TONY McCAULEY and MICHAEL D'ABO

Moderately fast rock shuffle ♩ = 126 (♫ = ♩♪)

Chorus:
C
E7
F
— me up, (build_ me up,) but - ter-cup, ba - by, just to let me down (let — me down) and
G7
C
E7
mess me a - round?_ And then worst — of all, (worst_ of all,) you nev - er call, ba - by, when you
F
G7
C
say you will. (say — you will.) But I love you, still. — I need you — (I need you_) more than an -
C/B♭
F/A
Dm7(♭5)/A♭
y - one, dar - ling. You know that I have from the start. — So,

C G Gsus G F C/E Dm7 C
build me up, (build_ me up,) but - ter - cup, don't break my heart._
Verse:
G7 C G7 B♭ F
1. I'll be o - ver at ten,_ you tell me time and a - gain,_ but you're late._
you, I'm a toy,_ but I could_ be the boy_ you a - dore,_
C F C G7
_ I wait a - round and then I run to the door._ I can't take_
_ if you'd just let me know. And though you're un - true,_ I'm at - tract -
B♭ F C F C/E Dm
_ an - y - more,_ it's not you._ You let me down a - gain.
ed to you_ all the more._ Why do I need you so?
(Hey, hey, hey._

G F Em
—) Ba - by, ba - by, try to find (hey, hey, hey, —) a lit - tle time and
A7 A G F D7 G7
I'll make you hap - py.
I'll make you mine. —
I'll — be home, I'll be be - side the phone, wait - ing for
3
you.
N.C.
Ooh, —
ooh... —
Chorus:
G7 C E7
Why do you build — me up, (build me up,) but - ter - cup, ba - by, just to

F G7 C
let me down (let me down) and mess me a - round? And then worst of all, (worst of all,) you
E7 F G7
nev - er call, ba - by, when you say you will. (say you will.) But I love you, still. I need you
C C/B♭ F/A
(I need you) more than an - y - one, dar - ling. You know that I have from the
Dm7(♭5)/A♭ C 1. G Gsus G
start. So, build me up, (build me up,) but - ter - cup, don't break my

2.
F C/E Dm7 C G7 G G7 G7sus G7
heart. 2. To ter - cup, don't break my
A A7 D
heart. I need you more than an -
D/C G/B Gm6/B♭
y - one, ba - by. You know that I have from the start. So,
D A Asus A G D/F♯ Em7 D
build me up, (build me up,) but - ter - cup, don't break my heart.

CARA MIA

Words and Music by
TULIO TRAPANI and LEE LANGE

Slowly and freely (♩ = 60)

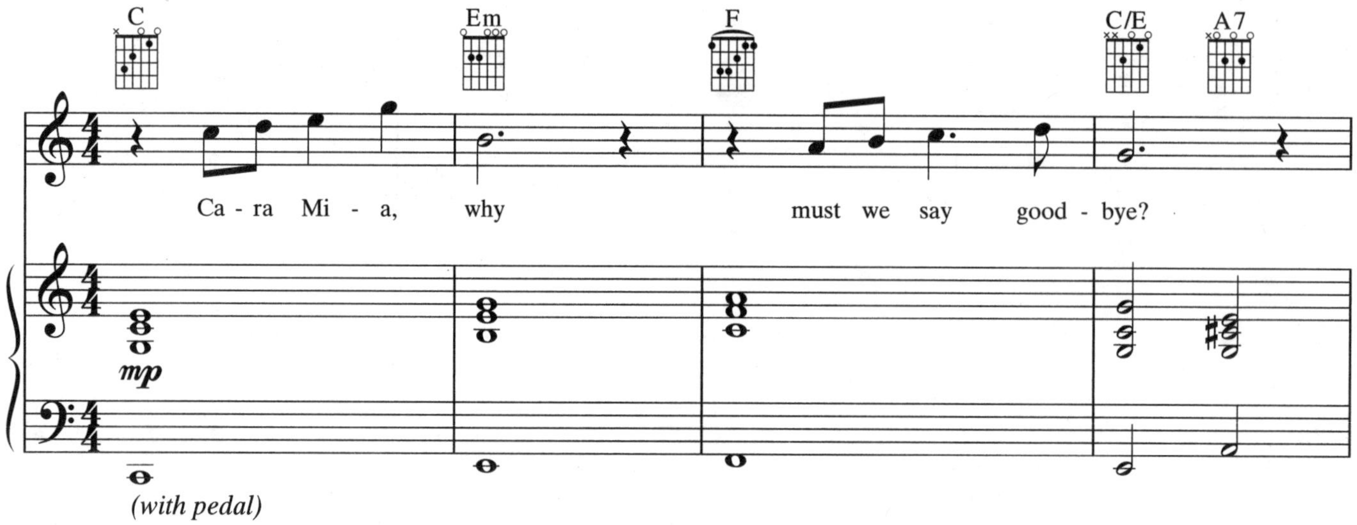

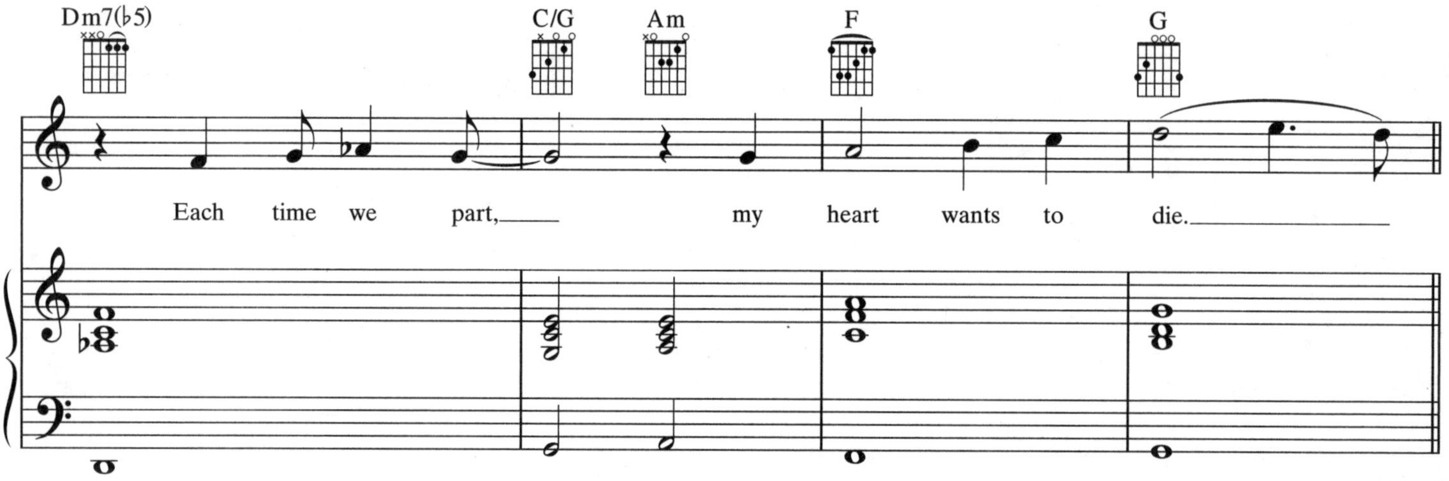

Moderate rock ♩ = 120

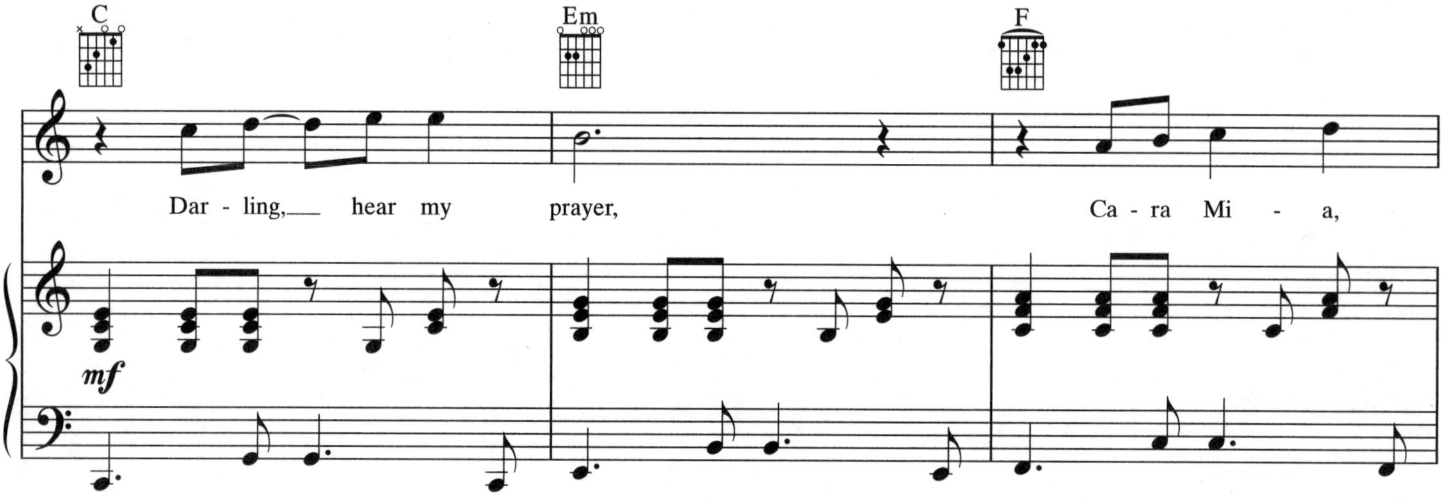

C Fm C Am
fair. I'll be your love till the
F G C
end of time.
Till the end of, till the end of, Ca - ra Mi - a mine,
Am F G F G
Ca - ra Mi - a mine, Ca - ra Mi - a mine, Ca - ra Mi - a mine.
C Em F
Ca - ra Mi - a, why must we say good -

C
Fm
C
Am
bye? Each time we part, my
F
G
C
heart wants to die.
Dar - ling, hear my
Em
F
C
prayer, Ca - ra Mi - a, fair.
Fm
C
Am
F
I'll be your love till the end
Till the end of,

G
C
Am
of
time.
till the end of,
Ca - ra Mi - a mine,
Ca - ra Mi - a mine,
F
G
C
Ca - ra Mi - a mine,
Ca - ra Mi - a mine.
Ah
Em
F
C
Ah.
ah.
Fm
C
Am
F
Each time we part,
my heart wants to

G
die.
Die.
C
Dar - ling, hear my
Em
F
C
prayer,
Ca - ra Mi - a,
fair.
Fm
C
Am
F
I'll be your love till the end
Till the end of,

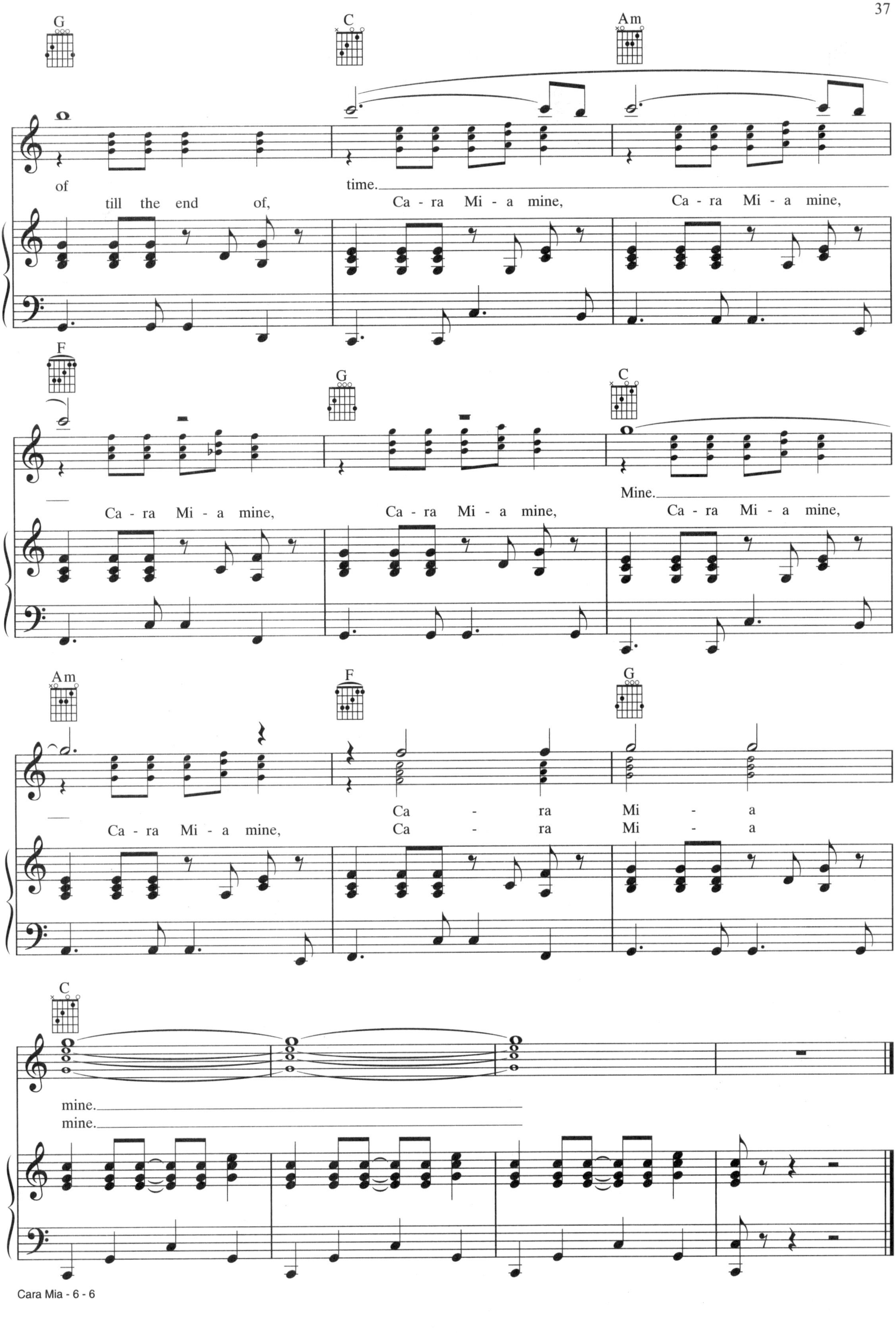
G
C
Am
of
time.
till the end of,
Ca - ra Mi - a mine,
Ca - ra Mi - a mine,
F
G
C
Mine.
Ca - ra Mi - a mine,
Ca - ra Mi - a mine,
Ca - ra Mi - a mine,
Am
F
G
Ca - ra Mi - a
Ca - ra Mi - a mine,
Ca - ra Mi - a
C
mine.
mine.

A CHANGE IS GONNA COME

Words and Music by
SAM COOKE

B♭
Cm7
E♭7
D7
long, a long time com-in', but I know, oh-oo-oh, a
Gm
1.
B♭
change gon' come, oh yes, it will. 2. It's been
2.
B♭
Verses 3 & 4:
B♭
yes, it will. 3. I go to the mov - ie and I
4. See additional lyrics
Cm7
go down - town. Some-bod-y keep tell-in' me don't

Gm
B♭
hang a - round. It's been a long, a long
Cm7
E♭7
D7
To Coda
Gm
time com-ing, but I know, oh-oo-oh, a change gon' come, oh
Bridge:
B♭
Cm7
yes, it will. Then I go, oh-oo-oh, to my
B♭6
Cm7
broth-er and I say, broth - er, help me

Verse 2:
It's been too hard living but I'm afraid to die
'Cause I don't know what's up there beyond the sky.
It's been a long, a long time comin',
But I know, oh-oo-oh,
A change gonna come, oh yes, it will.

Verse 4:
There've been times that I thought
I couldn't last for long
But now I think I'm able to carry on
It's been a long, a long time comin',
but I know, oh-oo-oh, a change gonna come, oh yes, it will.

CHAIN GANG

Words and Music by
SAM COOKE

Chorus:
G C G Em
know? That's the sound of the men work-in' on the chain gang,
G C D G
1.
that's the sound of the men work-in' on the chain gang. All day long they're say-in'…
2.
Verse 1:
G Em C
1. All day long they work so hard till the sun is go-in'
D G Em C
down, work-in' on the high-ways and by-ways and wear-ing, wear-ing a
3

D G Em C
frown. You hear them moan-in' their lives a-way,_ then_ you hear_
Chorus:
D G C G
some-bod-y say..._ That's the sound of the men work-in' on the chain
Em G C D G
gang,_ that's the sound of the men work-in' on the chain gang._
Verse 2:
G Em
_ 2. Can't you hear them say-in', mm? I'm_ go-in' home_ one of
(Huh.
Ha.

C D G
these days, I'm go-in' home, see my wom-an whom I love
Huh. Ha. Huh.
Em C D
so dear, but mean-while I've got to work right here.
8vb
Ha. Huh. Ha.) Well, don't you
Chorus:
G C G Em
(8vb) know? That's the sound of the men work-in' on the chain gang.
G C D G
That's the sound of the men work-in' on the chain gang. All day long they're say-in',

G Em C
mm. My, my, my, my, my, my, my. My
(Huh. Ha. Huh.
D G Em
work is so hard. Give me wa - ter, I'm thirst - y, my, my,
Ha. Huh. Ha.
C D G
my, my, my work is so hard. My, my, my, my,
Huh. Ha. Huh.
Em C D
Repeat ad lib. and fade
my, my, my, my, my work is so hard.
Ha. Huh. Ha.)

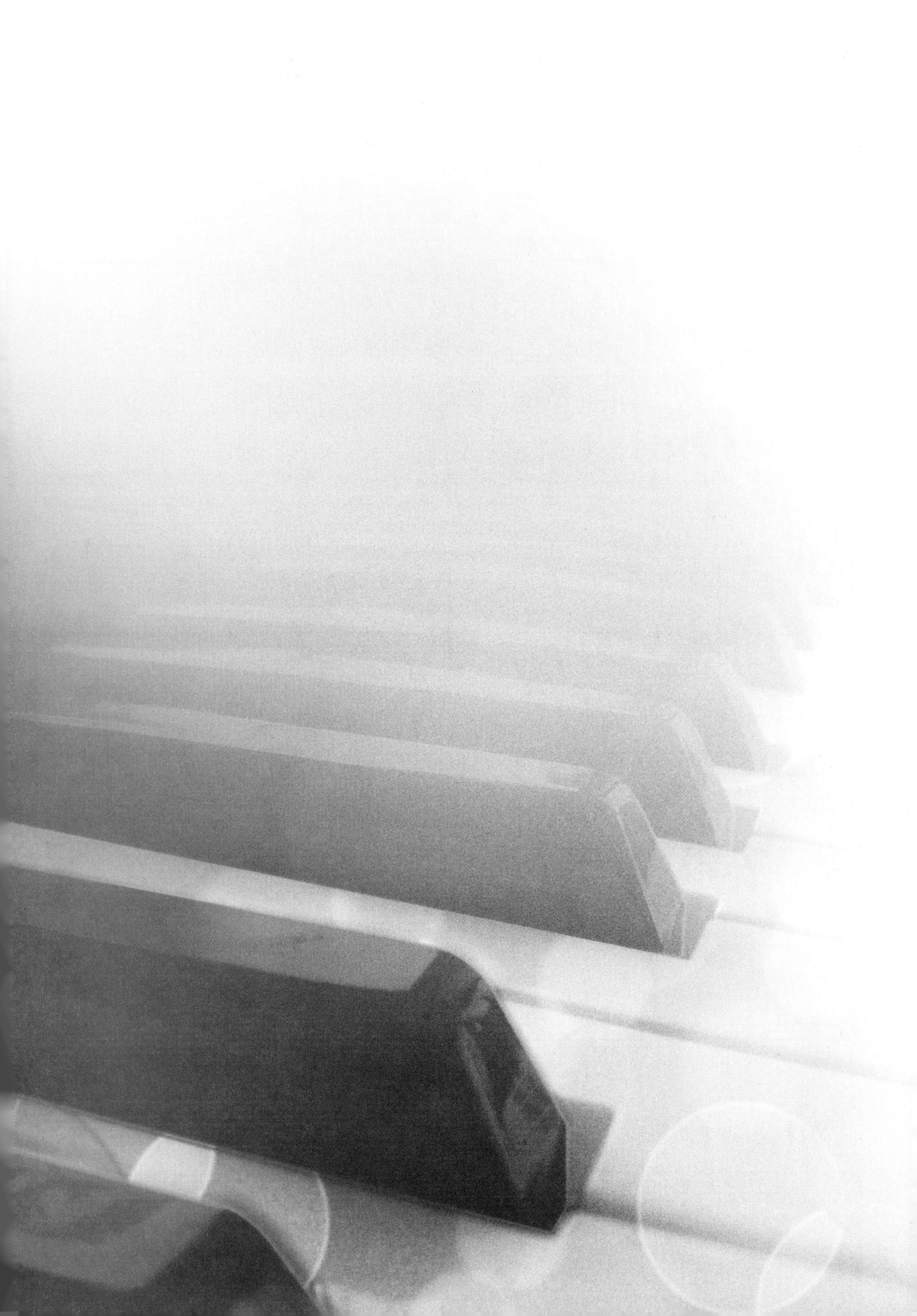

DO YOU WANT TO KNOW A SECRET

Words and Music by
JOHN LENNON and
PAUL McCARTNEY

* Original recording in E.

To Coda
B♭ C7 Dm
hear, I'm in love with you. Ooh.
1. 2.
Bridge:
Gm C7 Gm C7 B♭ Dm Cm
I've known a se-cret 'bout a week or two;
mp
D.S. al Coda
B♭ Dm Cm Gm C7
No-bod-y knows, just we two.
Coda
Gm C7 Dm Gm C7 Dm
Repeat and fade
Ooh. Ooh.

EASY TO BE HARD

(as recorded by Three Dog Night)

Music by GALT MacDERMOT
Words by JAMES RADO and GEROME RAGNI

Moderately slow ♩ = 86

Em7
A7
D
Dmaj7
D7
eas - y to be cold.
Verses 2 & 3:
Cmaj7
A7
Cmaj7
2. How can peo-ple have no feel - ings? How can they ig -
3. How can peo-ple be so heart - less? You know I'm hung
A7
Dmaj7
Em7
A7
nore their friends? Eas - y to be proud, eas -
up on you.
D
Dmaj7
D7
Bridge:
G
Dm7
y to say no.
'Spec - 'ly peo - ple who
mf

G Dm7 G Dm7 G Dm7
care a-bout strang-ers, who care a-bout e - vil and so-cial in-jus - tice.
Em7 A7 Em7 A7 Em7 A7
Do you on - ly care a-bout the bleed-ing crowd? How a - bout a
1. Dmaj7 Cmaj7 2. Dmaj7
need-ed friend? I need a friend.
need-ed friend? We all need a friend.
mp
Verse 4:
Cmaj7 Cmaj7 A7
4. How can peo-ple be so heart-less?

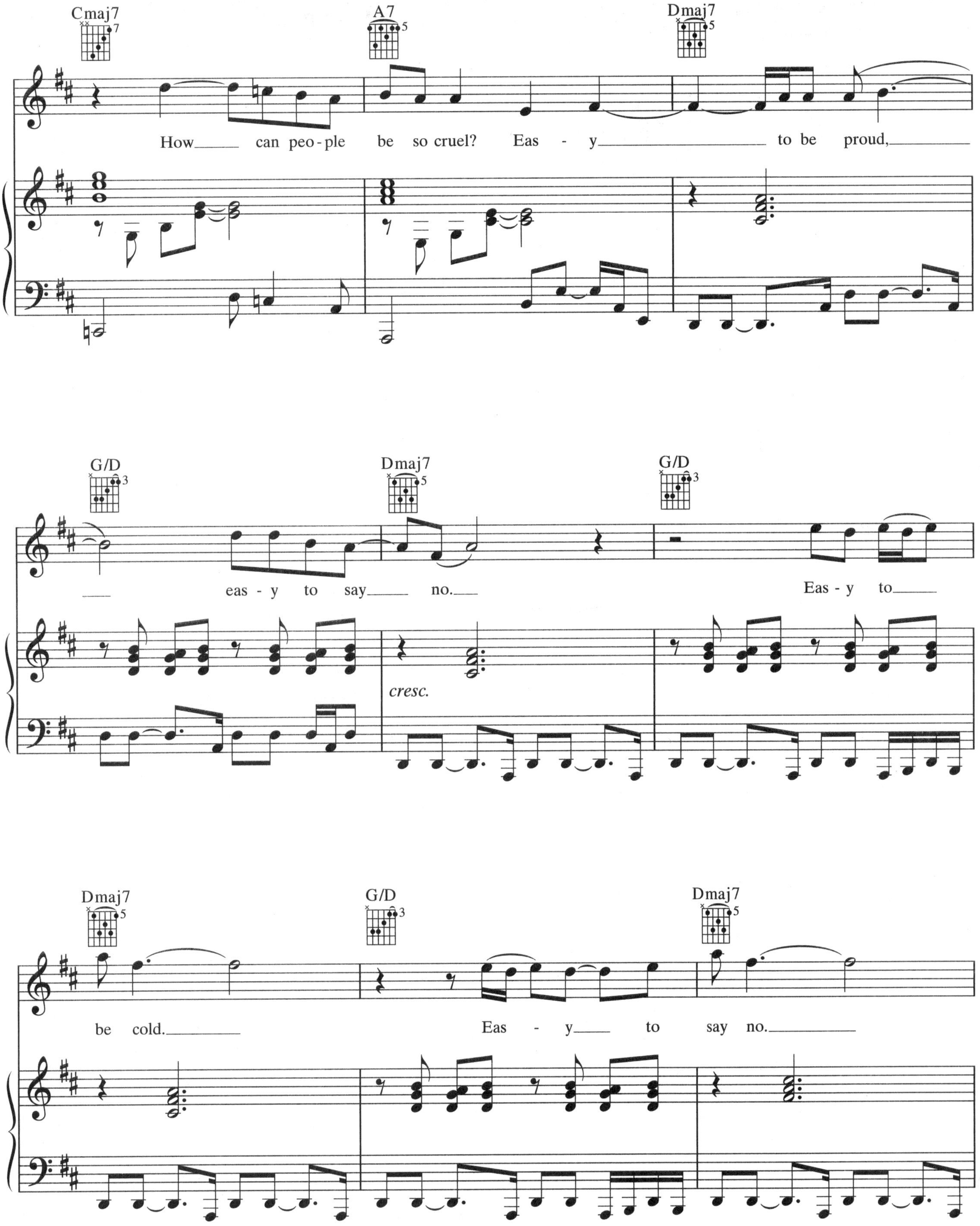
Cmaj7
A7
Dmaj7
How can peo-ple be so cruel? Eas - y to be proud,
G/D
Dmaj7
G/D
eas - y to say no.
Eas - y to
cresc.
Dmaj7
G/D
Dmaj7
be cold.
Eas - y to say no.

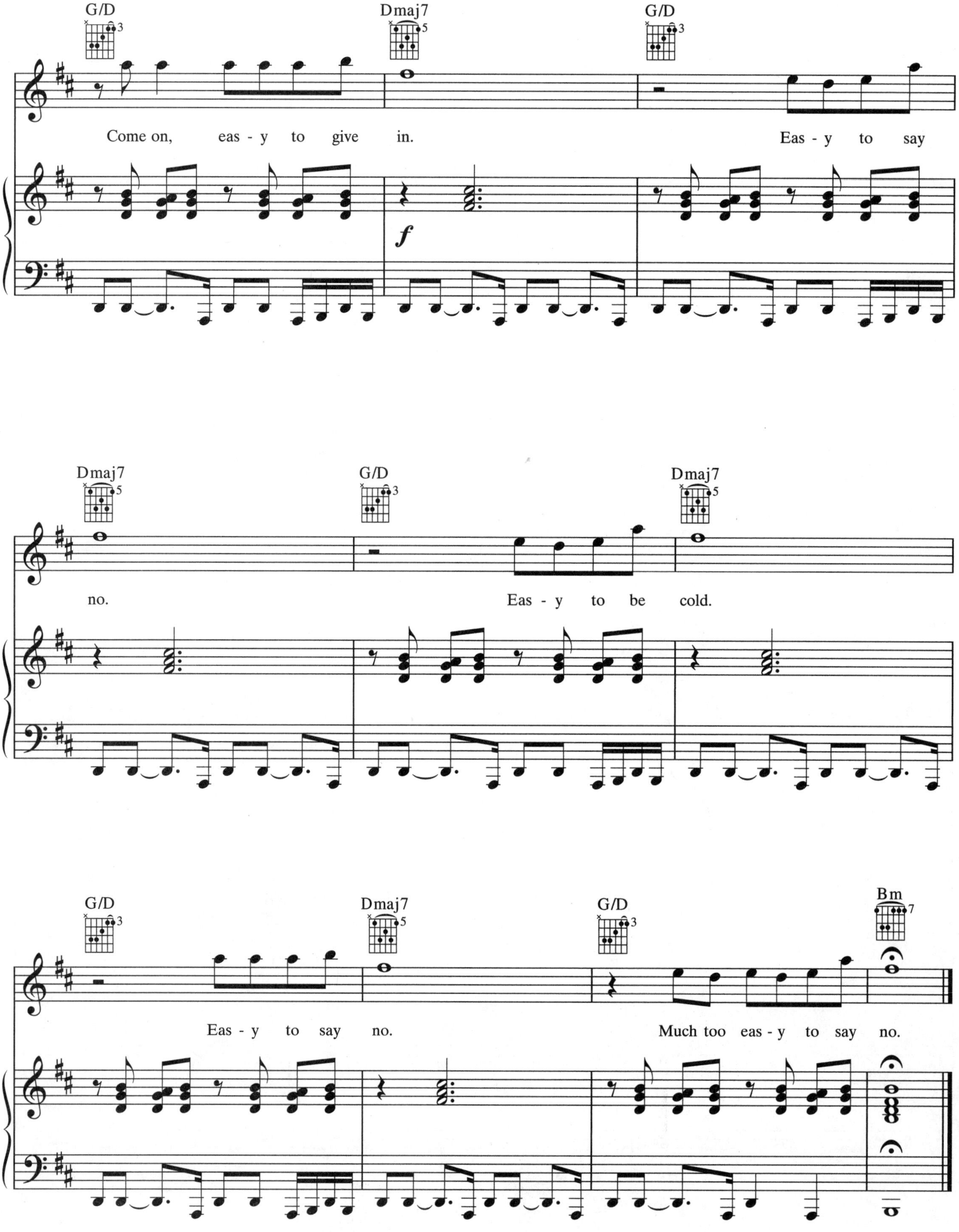
G/D
Dmaj7
G/D
Come on, eas - y to give in. Eas - y to say
Dmaj7
G/D
Dmaj7
no. Eas - y to be cold.
G/D
Dmaj7
G/D
Bm
Eas - y to say no. Much too eas - y to say no.

EIGHT MILES HIGH

Words and Music by
GENE CLARK, DAVID CROSBY and JIM McGUINN

Moderately ♩ = 128

Verse:
Em
F♯m7
G
D
1. Eight miles high and when you touch
2. No - where is there warmth to be
3. 'Round the squares, hud - dled in
3
C
G
D
down you'll find that it's - stran - ger than
found a - mong those a - fraid of los - ing their
storms, some laugh - ing, some just shape - less
C(9)
C
C(9)
Em
F♯m7
known. Signs in the
ground. Rain gray
forms. Side - walk

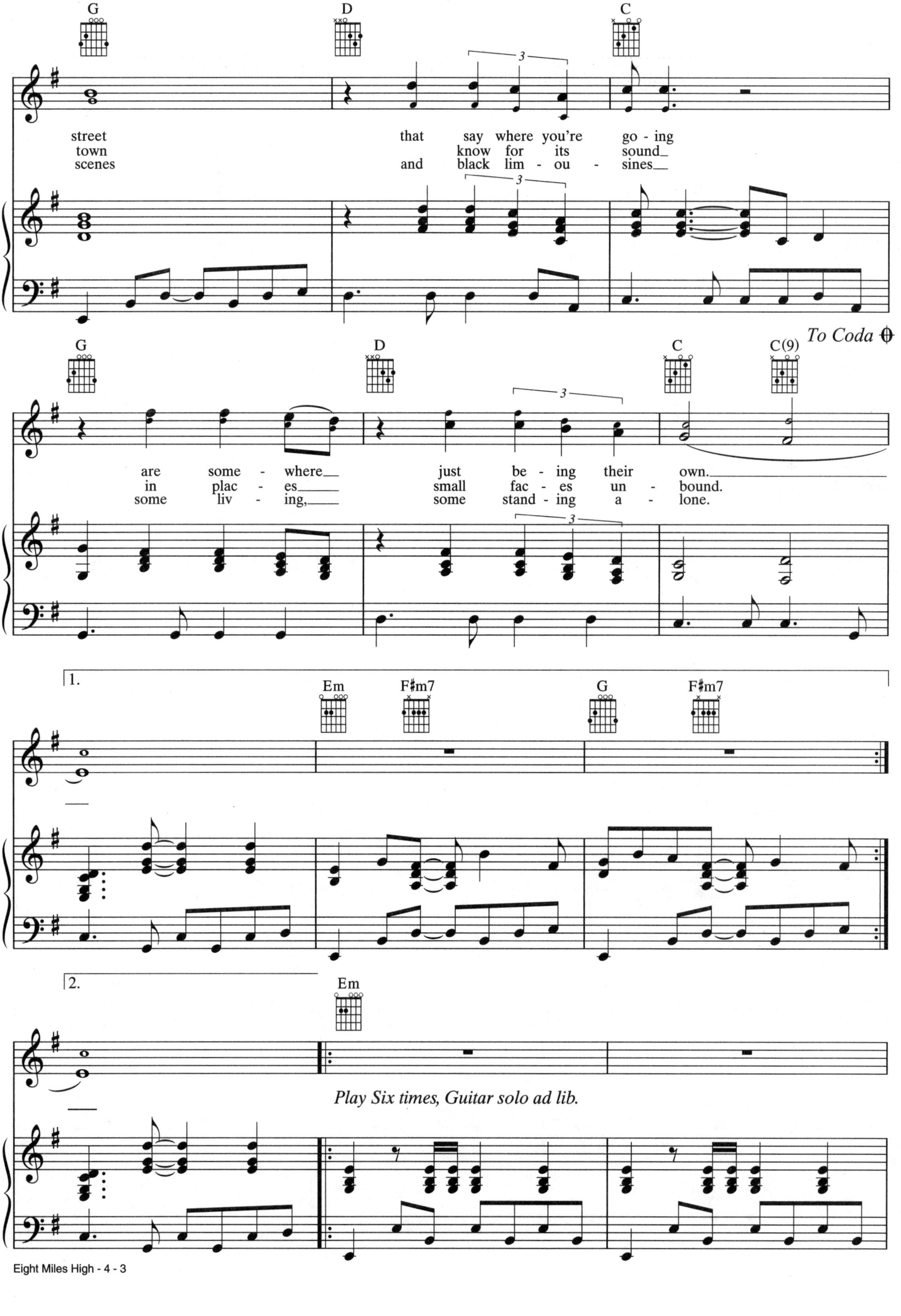
G D C
street that say where you're go - ing
town know for its sound
scenes and black lim - ou - sines
G D C C(9)
To Coda
are some - where just be - ing their own.
in plac - es small fac - es un - bound.
some liv - ing, some stand - ing a - lone.
1.
Em F♯m7 G F♯m7
2.
Em
Play Six times, Guitar solo ad lib.

D.S 𝄋 al Coda
𝄌 Coda
Em
F♯m7
Em
F♯m7
Guitar solo, repeat as desired
Em
F♯m7
Em
F♯m7
Em

THE END OF THE WORLD

Words and Music by
ARTHUR KENT and SYLVIA DEE

Slow ballad ♩. = 69

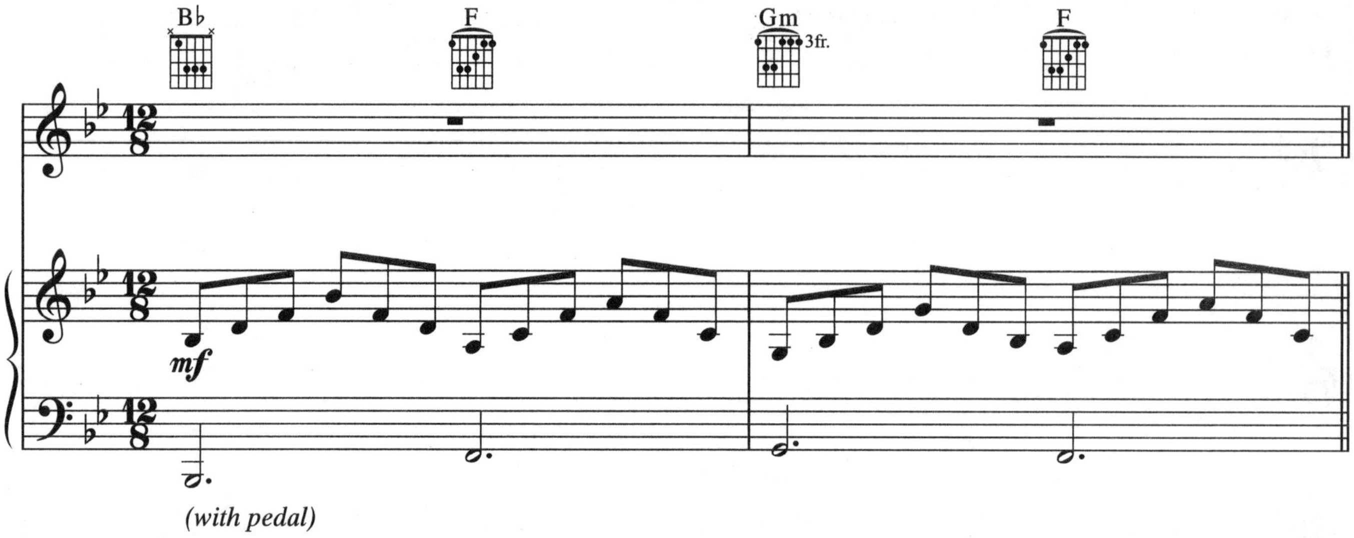

Verse 1:

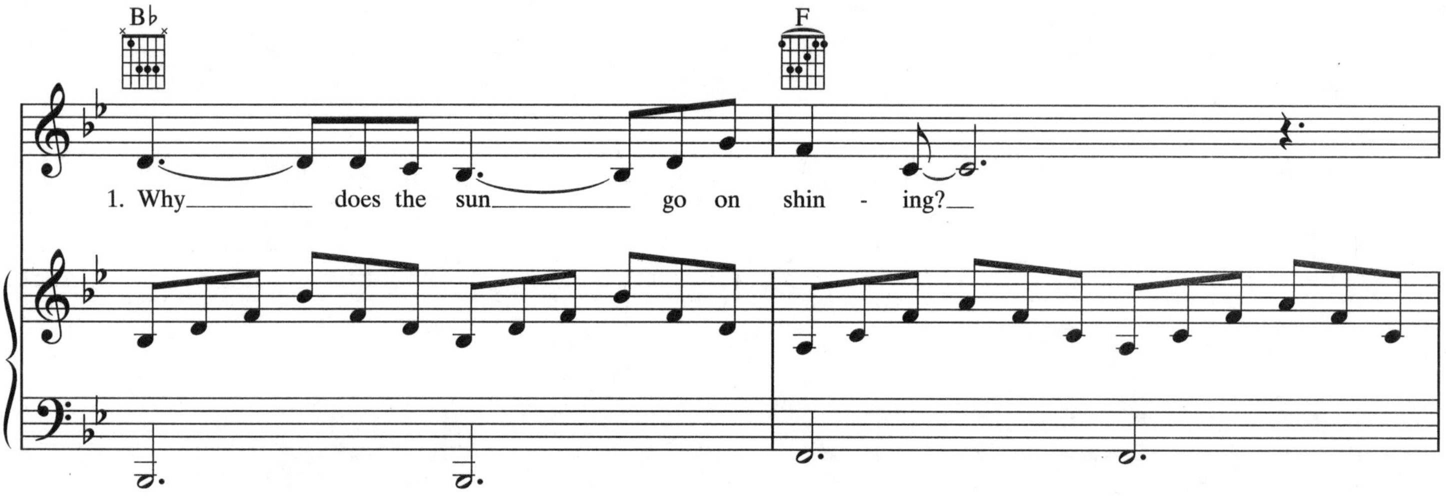

E♭
Cm
3fr.
Dm
G9
Don't they know it's the end of the world, 'cause
Cm
3fr.
E♭m
F
you don't love me an - y - more?
B♭
F
Why do the birds go on sing - ing?
Gm
3fr.
Dm
Why do the stars glow a - bove?

E♭ Cm 3fr. Dm G9
Don't they know it's the end of the world? It
Cm 3fr. F B♭
end - ed when I lost your love. I
Bridge:
E♭ B♭
wake up in the mor - ning and I won - der why
F B♭
ev - 'ry - thing's the same as it was; I

Dm
G9
can't un - der - stand, no I can't un - der - stand how
Cm
3fr.
E♭m
F
life goes on the way it does.
Verse 2:
B♭
F
2. Why ___ does my heart go on beat - ing? ___
Gm
3fr.
Dm
Why ___ do these eyes ___ of mine ___ cry? ___

E♭
Cm
3fr.
Dm
G9
Don't they know it's the end of the world? It
Cm
3fr.
F
B♭
F♯7
ended when you said goodbye.
B
F♯
(Spoken:) Why does my heart go on beating?
(Bkgrd.) Ooh.
G♯m
4fr.
D♯m
Why do these eyes of mine cry?
Ooh.

E
C#m
4fr.
D#m
G#9
3fr.
Don't they know it's the end of the world? It
C#m
4fr.
F#
B
D#m
end - ed when you said good - bye.
molto rit.
a tempo
E
F#7
B
rit.

FRIDAY ON MY MIND

Words and Music by
HARRY VANDA and GEORGE YOUNG

D
G
me. Com-ing Tues-day, I feel
me more than work-ing for the rich
B
E7
bet-ter. E-ven my
man. Hey, I'll change
Am
old man looks good.
that scene one day.
A7
Dm
Wednes-day just don't go. Thurs-day goes
To-day I might feel mad. To-mor-row I'll

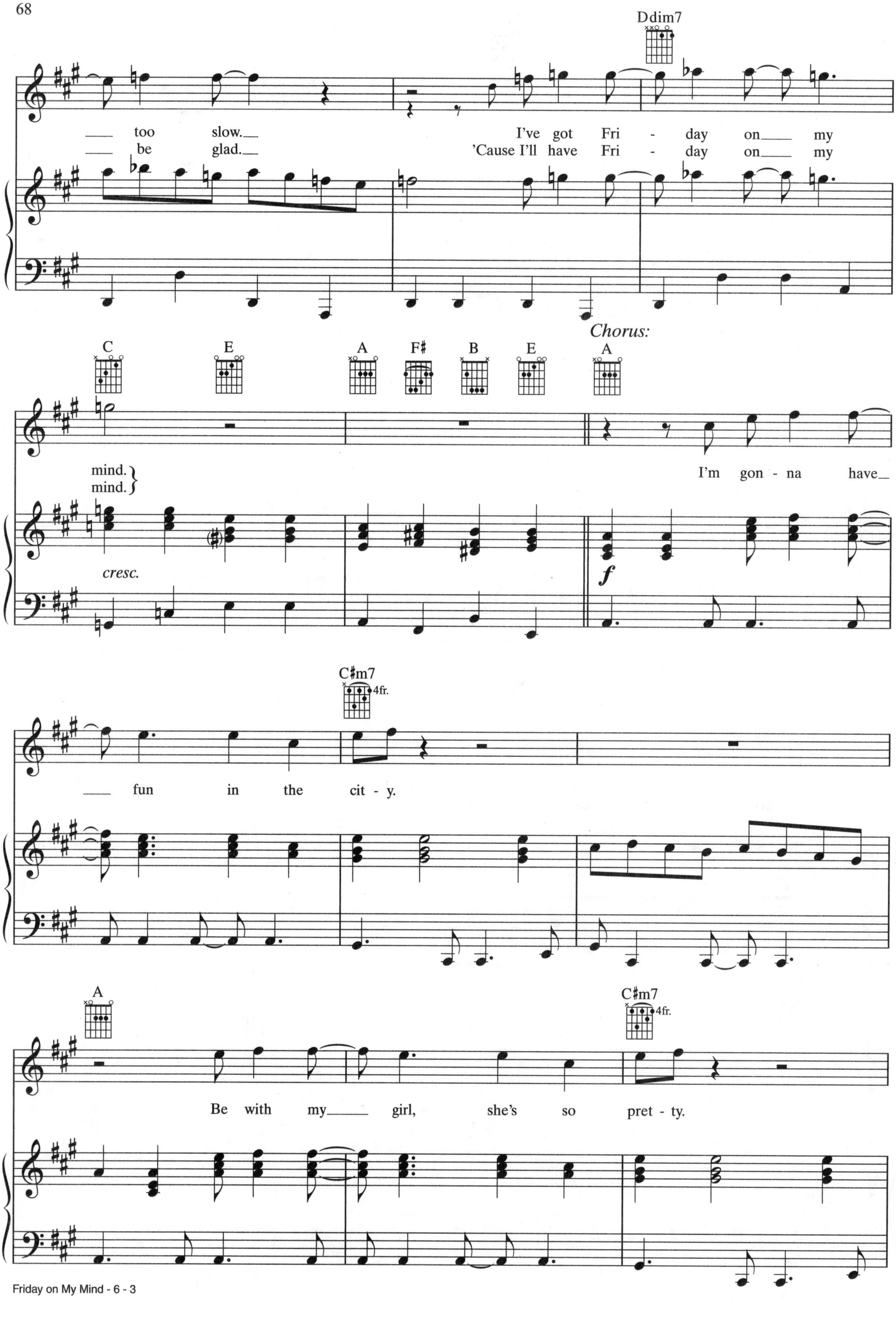
Ddim7
too slow. I've got Fri - day on my
be glad. 'Cause I'll have Fri - day on my
C E A F♯ B E
Chorus:
A
mind.
mind.
I'm gon - na have
cresc.
f
C♯m7
fun in the cit - y.
A C♯m7
Be with my girl, she's so pret - ty.

D
She looks fine to - night.
F♯
Bm
She is out of sight to me.
D
To - night I'll spend my bread. To - night
B
D
I'll lose my head. To - night I've

A/E
got to get to - night.
E7
Am
Mon - day I'll have
D/A
G/A
3fr.
1.
E7 N.C.
D.C.
2.
E7 N.C.
Fri - day on my mind.
(Drums)
(Drums)

Chorus:
A
I'm gon - na have___ fun in the
C♯m7
4fr.
cit - y.
A
I'll be with my__
__ girl, she's so pret - ty.
C♯m7
4fr.
Repeat ad lib. and fade

GOING UP THE COUNTRY

Words and Music by
ALAN WILSON

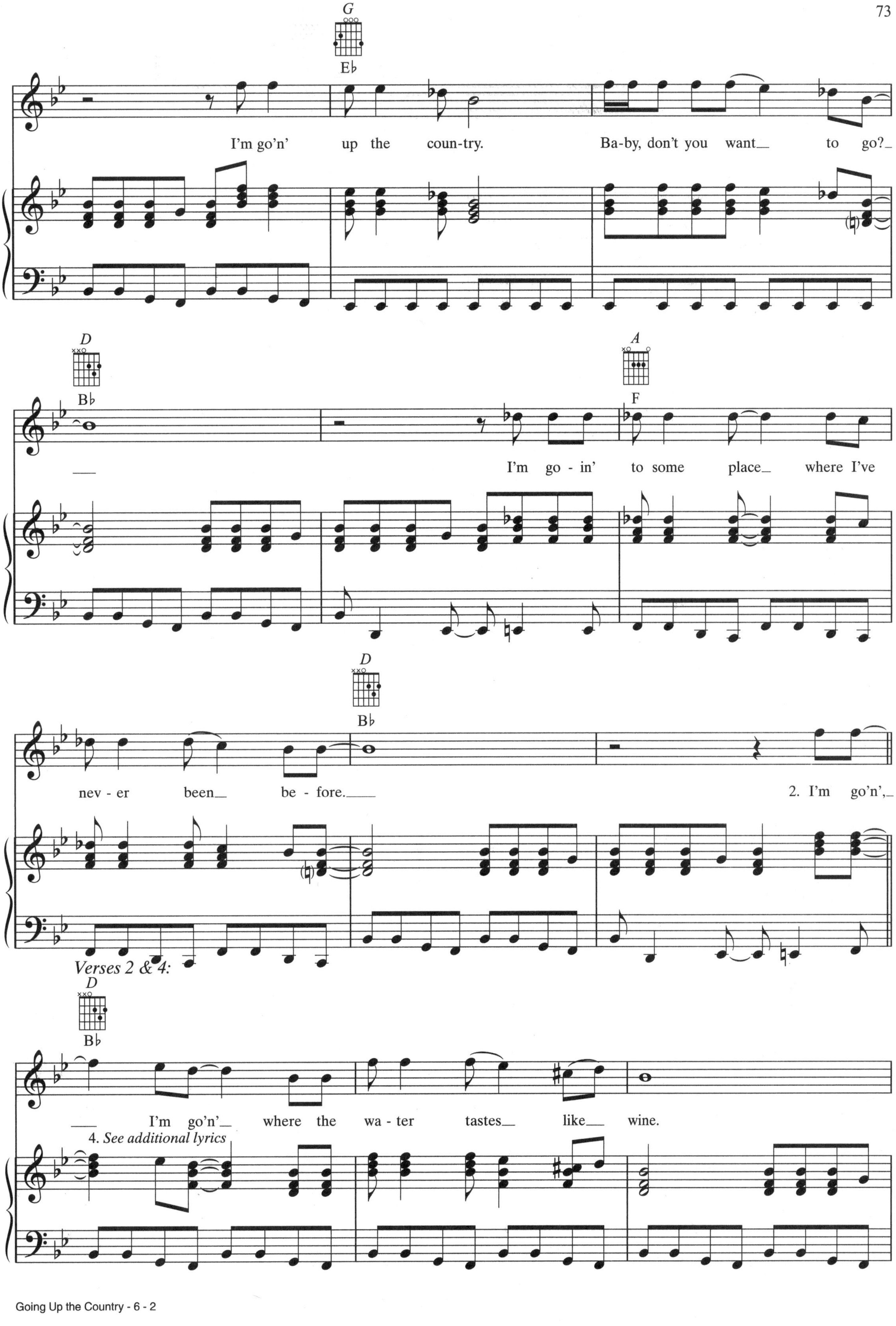
G
E♭
I'm go'n' up the coun-try. Ba-by, don't you want_ to go?_
D
B♭
A
F
_ I'm go-in' to some place_ where I've
D
B♭
nev-er been_ be-fore._ 2. I'm go'n',_
Verses 2 & 4:
D
B♭
_ I'm go'n'_ where the wa-ter tastes_ like_ wine.
4. See additional lyrics

G
E♭
I'm go - ing where the wa - ter tastes like
D
B♭
wine.
We can
A
F
jump in the wa - ter;
stay drunk all the time.
D
B♭
D
B♭

G
E♭
D
B♭
A
F
D
B♭
1.
3. I'm gon - na leave
2.
Tag:
G
E♭
No use in you run - ning,
or scream - ing and

D
B♭
A
F
cry'n', 'cause you got a home as
D
B♭
long as I got mine.
G
E♭
D
B♭
A
F
D
B♭

Verse 3:
I'm gonna leave the city
Got to get away.
I'm gonna leave the city
Got to get away.
All this fussin' and fightin;
Man, you know I sure can't stay.

Verse 4:
Now, baby pack your leavin' trunk
You know we've got to leave today.
Just exactly where we're goin' I cannot say
But we might even leave the USA
'Cause it's a brand new game
And I want to play.
(*To Tag:*)

ELUSIVE BUTTERFLY

Words and Music by
BOB LIND

Moderately bright 𝅗𝅥 = 96

Fm/E♭
Dm/C
up some morn - ing___ to the sound_
heard my foot - steps___ ech - o soft -
B♭
G
Fm
Dm
E♭maj7
Cmaj7
___ of some-thing mov - ing past your win - dow in___ the wind._
ly in the dis - tance through the can - yons of___ your mind._
Fm
Dm
___ And, if___ you're quick e - nough_ to rise,_
___ I might_ have e - ven called_ your name_
B♭7
G7
Fm
Dm
B♭7
G7
___ you'll catch the fleet - ing glimpse_ of some - one's fad - ing
___ as I ran search - ing af - ter some - thing to be -

E♭maj7
Cmaj7
shad - ow.
lieve in.
Fm/E♭
Dm/C
Out on the new ho - ri - zon,
You might have seen me run - ning
B♭
G
Fm
Dm
you may see the float - ing mo - tion of a
through the long a - ban - doned ru - ins of the
E♭maj7
Cmaj7
dis - tant pair of wings. And, if the
dreams you left be - hind. If you re -

Fm
Dm
B♭7
G7
Fm
Dm
sleep has left___ your ears,___ you might___ hear foot - steps run - ning
mem - ber some - thing there___ that glid - ed past you, fol - lowed
B♭7
G7
E♭maj7
Cmaj7
through an o - pen mead - ow.___
close by heav - y breath - ing.___
Chorus:
Fm
Dm
Don't be con - cerned,___
B♭7
G7
E♭maj7
Cmaj7
E♭6
C6
it will___ not harm___ you.___ It's on - ly

Fm
Dm
B♭7
G7
E♭maj7
Cmaj7
me pur - su - ing some - thing I'm not sure of.
E♭6
C6
Fm
Dm
B♭7
G7
A - cross my dream, with nets of
E♭maj7
Cmaj7
E♭6
C6
Fm
Dm
won - der, I chase the bright e - lus - ive
B♭7
G7
E♭maj7
Cmaj7
1.
but - ter - fly of love.

2.
Fm
Dm
B♭7
G7
(Strings)
E♭maj7
Cmaj7
E♭6
C6
Fm
Dm
B♭7
G7
E♭maj7
Cmaj7
E♭6
C6
Fm
Dm
B♭7
G7
E♭maj7
Cmaj7

Eb6
C6
Fm
Dm
Bb7
G7
Ebmaj7
Cmaj7
Fm
Dm
A - cross my dream,
Bb7
G7
Ebmaj7
Cmaj7
Eb6
C6
with nets of won - der, I chase the
Fm
Dm
Bb7
G7
Ebmaj7
Cmaj7
bright e - lus - ive but - ter - fly of love.

GOLDFINGER

Lyric by LESLIE BRICUSSE
and ANTHONY NEWLEY

Music by JOHN BARRY

Moderately (♩ = 104)

* Original recording in E.

E
Am
Am(♯5)
Am6
Am(♯5)
sin, but don't go in. Gold-en
Em
Am7
B7
Em
B7(♯9)
words he will pour in your ear, but his lies can't dis-guise what you fear. For a
E
Cm
C7
D♭dim7
gold - en girl knows when he's kissed her. It's the kiss of death from Mis - ter
F
D♭
Cm
F
B♭
Gold - fin-ger. Pret-ty girl, be - ware of this heart of

1.
2.
E
Am Am(♯5) Am6 Am(♯5) Am Am(♯5)
gold. This heart is cold. Gold - en cold.
Am6 Am(♯5) Am Am(♯5) Am6 Am(♯5) Am Am(♯5) Am6 Am(♯5)
He love's on - ly gold, on - ly gold. He loves
Am Am(♯5) Am Am(♯5) Am6 Am(♯5) Am Am(♯5) Am Am(♯5) Am Am(♯5)
gold. He love's on - ly gold, on - ly gold. He loves
Am6
gold.

GOOD MORNING STARSHINE

(from *Hair*)

Lyrics by
JAMES RADO and
GEROME RAGNI

Music by
GALT MacDERMOT

Verse:

Eb F Eb F Eb F
star - shine. The earth says hel - lo.
star - shine. There's love in your skies,
Eb F Eb F Eb F
3
You twin - kle a - bove us, we twin - kle
re - flect - ing the sun - light in my lov -
Bb Eb F Eb F
be - low. Good morn - ing, star - shine.
er's eyes. Good morn - ing, star - shine.
Eb F Eb F Eb D
You lead us a - long, my love and
So hap - py to see my love and

Gm B♭7 E♭ B♭m C7 F7
me, as___ we___ sing___ our ear - ly morn - ing
me, as___ we___ sing___ our ear - ly morn - ing
B♭
Chorus:
sing - ing song.
sing - ing song.
Glid - dy gloop gloo - py nib - by nab - by noo - py la
Cm7 F7 Cm7 F7 Cm7
la la lo lo.___
Sab - ba sib - by sab - ba noo -
F7sus F7 B♭ B♭7
by ab - ba nab - ba lee___ lee lo lo.___

E♭ D Gm Cm B♭ F7
Noo - by oo - by wad - da noo - by ab - ba nab - ba. Ear - ly morn - ing sing - ing song.
1. 2.
B♭ N.C. B♭ N.C. A♭
2. Good morn - ing,
E♭ F E♭ F E♭ F
Can you hear me?

E♭ F B♭
Sing - ing a song,
lov - ing a song,
Cm7 F7 Cm7 F7 F7sus
sing - ing a song.
Lov - ing a song,
laugh -
F7 B♭ B♭7
ing a song,
sing - ing a song.
E♭ D Gm Cm B♭ Gm7
Sing a song,
song a sing,
song, song, song, sing,

Cm7 F7 B♭ B♭maj7 B♭6 B♭
sing, sing, sing, song.
B♭ Gm7 Cm7 F7 B♭ B♭maj7
Song, song, song, sing, sing, sing, sing, song.
B♭6 B♭
Sing a sing song, sing a song.
(Continue ad lib. vocals)
B♭ B♭maj7
1.2. B♭6 B♭
3. B♭6 B♭
Sing.

GREEN TAMBOURINE

Words and Music by
SHELLEY PINZ and PAUL LEKA

*Harmony vocals sung 3rd verse.

To Coda
1.
2.
D.C. al Coda
G
D
C
G
D
C
G
D
C
ine.
Coda
G
D
C
G7
C/G
G
B♭
Fm/A♭
List - en and I'll play...

HAIR

Words by
JAMES RADO and
GEROME RAGNI

Music by
GALT MacDERMOT

Moderately ♩ = 92
N.C.
mf
(with pedal)
Freely, slowly
(Bkgrd.) She asked__ him__ why.
E♭
Male:
Why__ I'm a hair - y guy.__
Cm
I'm hair - y noon_ and

Eb
night-y night night. My hair is a fright.
Gm Eb Gm Bb
I'm hair-y high and low. But don't ask me why. (Bkgrd.) 'Cause he don't know.
Gm Eb Gm Bb Ab Bb N.C.
It's not for lack of bread like the Grate-ful Dead, dar-ling.
(Drums)
Moderately ♩ = 108
Verses 1 & 3:
Cm Ab Cm Eb Cm Ab
1.3. Give me a head with hair, long beau-ti-ful hair. Shin-ing, gleam-ing,

Cm Eb Gm Eb Gm Bb
stream-ing, flax-en, wax-en. Give me down to there,_ (hair) shoul-der length or long-er. (hair)
Gm Eb Gm Bb
Here, ba-by, there, ma-ma, ev-'ry-where, dad-dy, dad-dy.
Chorus:
Cm Ab/C Cm Eb
Hair._ Grow it,
Hair, hair, hair, hair, hair, hair. Oh,
Bb Eb7 Ab Bb
To Coda N.C.
show it, long_ as I can grow it, my hair. 2. I'd let it
ah, oo, love my hair.

Verse 2:
Cm
Ab
Cm
Eb
Cm
Ab
fly in the breeze_ and get caught in the trees,_ give a home___ for the fleas_ in my
Cm
Gm
Eb
Gm
Bb
hair. A home for the fleas,_ a hive for the buzz-in' bees. A
Gm
Eb
Gm
Bb
nest for birds, there ain't no words for the beau - ty, the splen - dor, the won - der of my
Chorus:
Cm
Ab
Cm
Eb
Hair.___
Hair, hair, hair, hair, hair, hair. Oh,
Grow it,

B♭
E♭7
A♭
B♭
E♭
Female:
ah, show it, oo, long love as I can grow it, my hair. my hair.
I want it
Bridge:
G7sus
G7
G7sus
G7
C7sus
C7
long, straight, cur - ly, fuz - zy snag - gy, shag - gy, rat - ty, mat - ty. Oil - y, greas - y, fleec - y, shin - ing,
C7sus
C7
B♭/C
F
B♭/C
F
gleam - ing, stream - ing, flax - en, wax - en. Knot - ted pol - ka - dot - ted, twist - ed, bead - ed, braid - ed.
B♭/C
F
B♭/C
F
B♭
Male:
Pow - dered, flow - ered, and con - fet - tied, mang - led, tang - led, spang - led and spa - ghet - tied.
Oh,

E♭
Cm
F7
say can you see my___ eyes, if you
B♭
N.C.
Cm
A♭
Cm
A♭
can then my hair's too short. Down to here, down to there. Down to there, down to where it
B♭
N.C.
D.S 𝄋 al Coda
stops by it - self. Don't nev - er have to cut it 'cause it stops by it - self. Oh,

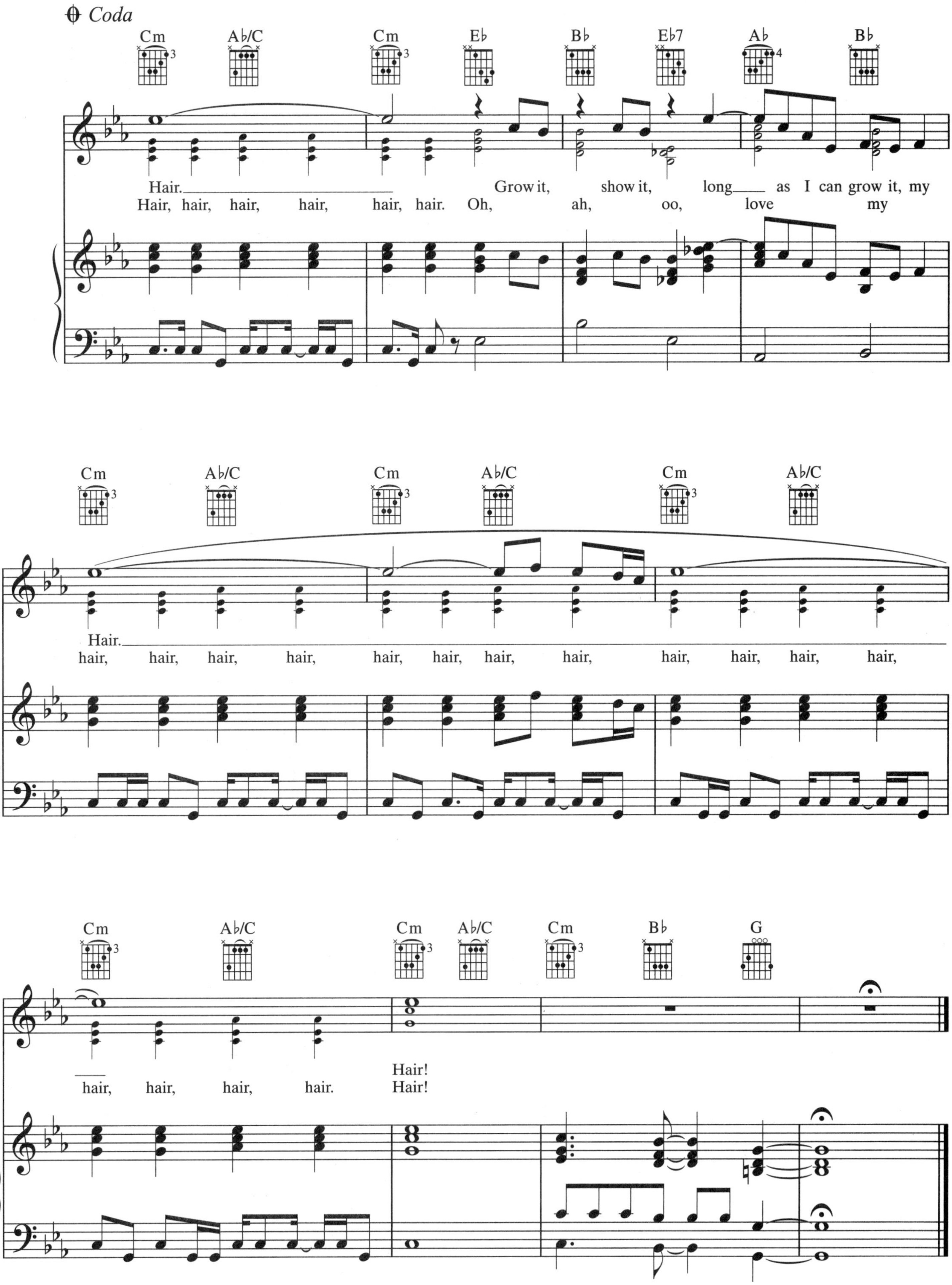
Coda
Cm Ab/C Cm Eb Bb Eb7 Ab Bb
Hair. Grow it, show it, long as I can grow it, my
Hair, hair, hair, hair, hair, hair. Oh, ah, oo, love my
Cm Ab/C Cm Ab/C Cm Ab/C
Hair.
hair, hair, hair, hair, hair, hair, hair, hair, hair, hair, hair, hair,
Cm Ab/C Cm Ab/C Cm Bb G
hair, hair, hair, hair. Hair!
Hair!

SWEET SOUL MUSIC

Words and Music by
SAM COOKE
Additional Material by ARTHUR CONLEY
and OTIS REDDING

Bright rock and roll ♩ = 160

Verse 1:
F
C
___ on the floor, ya'll,_ a - go - in' to a go - go, danc -
(Bkgrd. vocals cont. sim. to end)
F
Am
G
F
C
in' with the mu - sic,__ oh yeah,___ oh,___ yeah._ 2. Spot - light_
Verses 2–4:
F
___ on Lou Rawls, ya'll.___ Oh, don't___ he look boss, ya'll,_
___ on Sam and Dave, ya'll. Oh, don't___ they look great, ya'll,_
___ on Wil-son Pick-ett, now that wick - ed, wick-ed Pick - ett,___
C
F
sing - in' "Love's___ A Hurt - in' Thing," ya'll,___ oh yeah,_
sing - in' "Hold___ On, I'm___ Com - in',"___ oh yeah,_
sing - in' "Mus - tang______ Sal - ly,"___ oh yeah,_

1.2.
3.
Am
G
F
C
F
C
___ oh,___ oh yeah.___ 3. Spot - light___ ___ 5. Spot - light_
___ oh,___ oh yeah.___ 4. Spot - light_
___ oh,___ oh yeah._
Verse 5:
F
___ on O - tis Red - ding now, sing - in' "Fa___ fa fa fa fa fa fa,__
C
F
___ ha, fa fa___ fa fa fa fa fa fa."___ Oh yeah,_

Am G F C
oh, oh yeah. Get it, O - tis.
F C F C F C N.C.
6. Spot - light
Verse 6:
F C
on James Brown, ya'll. He's the king of them all, ya'll. He's the king
F Am G F C
of them all, ya'll, oh yeah, oh, oh yeah. Do you like

Chorus:
F
C
good music? That sweet soul mu - sic? Just long
F
Am
G
F
C
as it's swing - in', oh yeah, oh, oh yeah. I got
to get the feel - in'. I got to get the feel - in'. Do you like
Repeat ad lib. and fade
good mu - sic? That sweet soul mu - sic? Do you like

JAMES BOND THEME
(from *Dr. No*)

By MONTY NORMAN

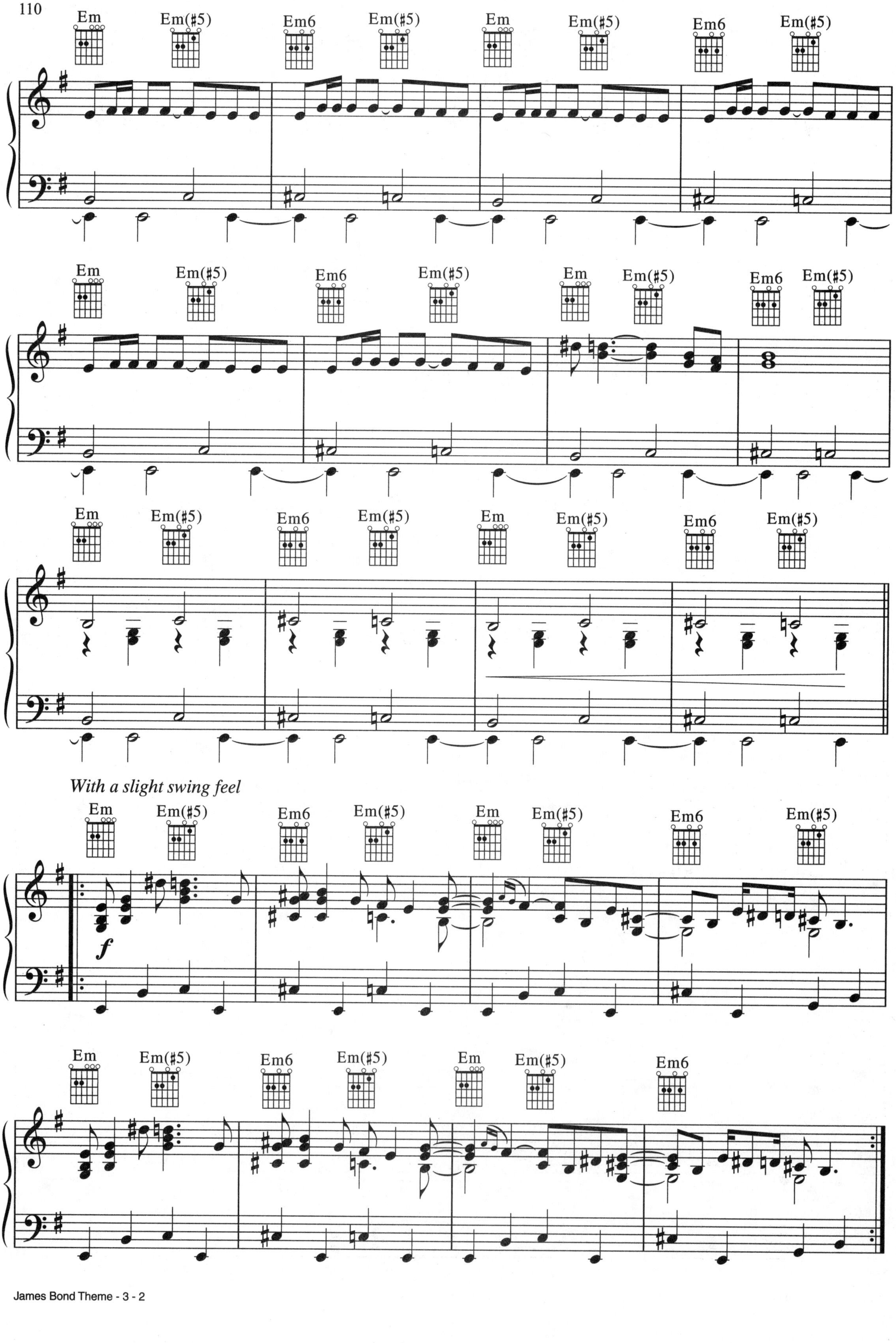
Em Em(♯5) Em6 Em(♯5) Em Em(♯5) Em6 Em(♯5)
Em Em(♯5) Em6 Em(♯5) Em Em(♯5) Em6 Em(♯5)
Em Em(♯5) Em6 Em(♯5) Em Em(♯5) Em6 Em(♯5)
With a slight swing feel
Em Em(♯5) Em6 Em(♯5) Em Em(♯5) Em6 Em(♯5)
f
Em Em(♯5) Em6 Em(♯5) Em Em(♯5) Em6

Em6
B9
Em
Em(♯5)
mf
N.C.
Em9(maj7)
7fr.
p

I SAW HER STANDING THERE

Words and Music by
JOHN LENNON and PAUL McCARTNEY

B7
E7
So how could I dance
She wouldn't dance
A
Am7/C
with an - oth - er, woah, when I
with an - oth - er, woah, when I
E7
B7
E7
saw her stand - ing there.
saw her stand - ing there.
1.
2.
Bridge:
A7
2. Well, she
Well, my heart went boom

when I crossed that room, and I
B7
held her hand in mine.
A7
3.4. Oh, we danced
Verses 3 & 4:
E7
A7
through the night and we held each oth - er tight.

E7
And be - fore too long, I fell in love with her.
B7
E7
Now, I'll nev - er dance
A
Am7/C
with an - oth - er, ooh,
{ when I / since I }
E7
B7
To Coda
E7
saw her stand - ing there.

Guitar solo:
3
B7
7
E7
5
A
5
Am
5

E7
B7
E7
D.S. 𝄋 al Coda
Well, my
𝄌 Coda
E7
Oh, since I saw her
B7
E7
stand - ing there.
Yeah, well, since I saw her
B7
A9
E7
E9
stand - ing there.

KIND OF A DRAG

Words and Music by
JAMES HOLVAY

Moderately fast rock ♩ = 138

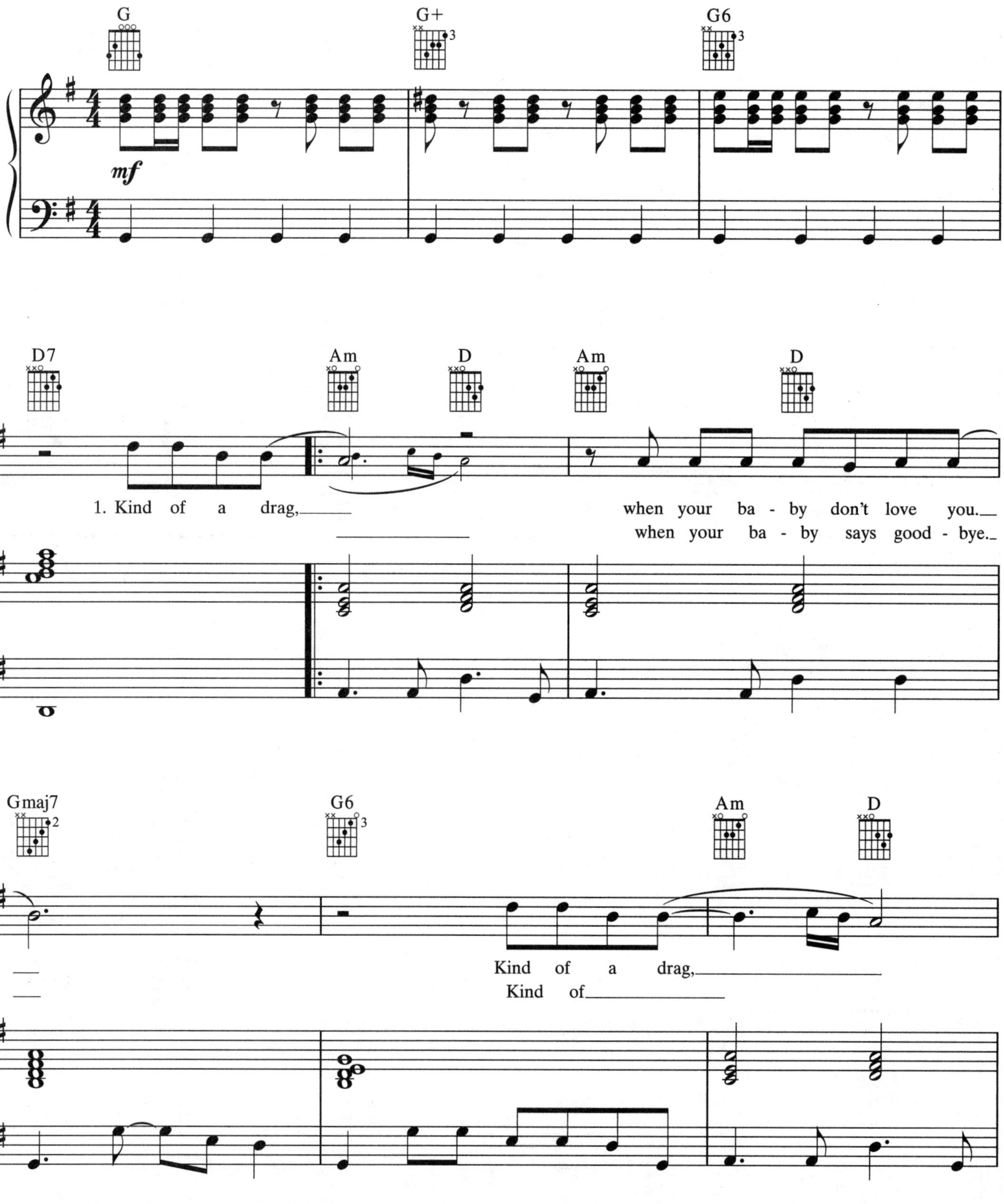
G
G+
G6
mf
D7
Am
D
Am
D
1. Kind of a drag,
when your ba - by don't love you.
when your ba - by says good - bye.
Gmaj7
G6
Am
D
Kind of a drag,
Kind of

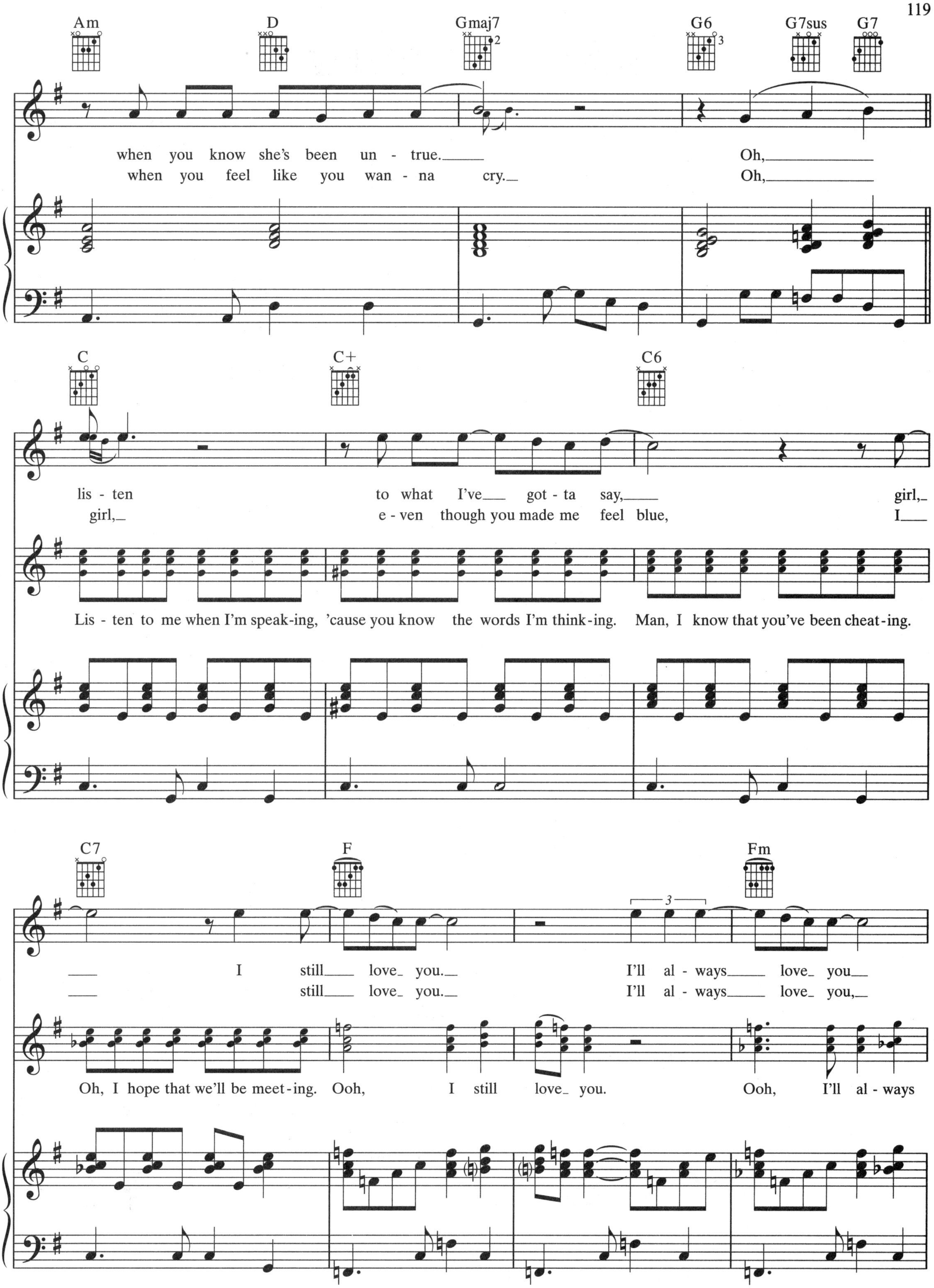
Am
D
Gmaj7
G6
G7sus
G7
when you know she's been un - true.
Oh,
when you feel like you wan - na cry.
Oh,
C
C+
C6
lis - ten
to what I've got - ta say,
girl,
girl,
e - ven though you made me feel blue,
I
Lis - ten to me when I'm speak - ing, 'cause you know the words I'm think - ing. Man, I know that you've been cheat - ing.
C7
F
Fm
I still love you.
I'll al - ways love you
still love you.
I'll al - ways love you,
Oh, I hope that we'll be meet - ing. Ooh, I still love you.
Ooh, I'll al - ways

C
B♭
C
3
an - y - way.
an - y - way.
An - y - way.
An - y - way.
love you.
Way.
Way.
B♭
C
1.
G
2.
G
3
An - y - way.
An - y - way.
2. Kind of a drag,
Way.
Am
D7
Am
D7
Gmaj7
G6

Am D7 Am D7 Gmaj7 G6 G7sus G7
Oh,
C C+ C6
lis-ten to what I've gotta say, girl,
Lis-ten to me when I'm speak-ing, 'cause you know the words I'm think-ing. Man, I know that you've been cheat-ing.
C7 F G/F F
I still love you. I'll al-ways
Oh, I hope that we'll be meet-ing. Ooh, I still love you.

Fm
F sus2 sus4
Fm
C
love you, an - y - way.
Ooh, I'll al - ways love you. Way.
B♭
C
B♭
Repeat ad lib. and fade
3
An - y - way. An - y
Way.

LAY LADY LAY

Moderately slow ♩ = 80

Words and Music by
BOB DYLAN

A C♯m G Bm A C♯m
Lay, la - dy, lay, lay a-cross my big brass bed.
Un-til the break of day, let me see you make him smile.
G Bm E F♯m A
What ev - er col - ors you have in your mind,
His clothes are dirt - y but his hands are clean.
E F♯m A
I'll show them to you and you'll see them shine.
And you're the best thing that he's ev - er seen.
A C♯m G Bm
Lay, la - dy, lay, lay a - cross my big brass bed.
Stay, la - dy, stay, stay with your man a - while.

1.
2.
A
C♯m
G
Bm
G
Bm
Bridge:
C♯m
E
F♯m
A
Why wait an - y long - er for the world to be - gin?
mf
C♯m
Bm
A
You can have your cake and eat it too.
C♯m
E
F♯m
A
Why wait an - y long - er for the one you love when he's stand -

C♯m
Bm
ing in front of you.
Verse 3:
A
C♯m
G
Bm
A
C♯m
3. Lay, la-dy, lay,
lay a-cross my big brass bed.
mp
G
Bm
A
C♯m
G
Bm
Stay, la-dy, stay,
stay while the night is still a-head.
A
C♯m
G
Bm
E
F♯m
I long to see you in the

A
E
F♯m
A
morn - ing light.
I long to reach for you
in the night.
A
C♯m
G
Bm
Stay, la - dy, stay,
stay while the night is still a - head.
A
C♯m
G
Bm
A
Bm
C♯m
D
A

LEAVING ON A JET PLANE

Words and Music by
JOHN DENVER

Moderately, with a light shuffle feel ♩ = 132

D Amaj7 F♯m7
side your door, I hate to wake you up to say good -
played a - round, I tell you now, they don't mean a
me kiss you, then close your eyes, I'll be on my
E7 A
bye. But the dawn is break - in', it's
thing. Ev - 'ry place I go, I'll
way. Dream a - bout the
D Amaj7 D
ear - ly morn, the tax - i's wait - in', he's blow - in' his horn. Al -
think of you, ev - 'ry song I sing, I'll sing for you, when
days to come, when I won't have to leave a - lone, a -
Amaj7 F♯m E7
read - y I'm so lone - some I could cry.
I come back, I'll wear your wed - ding ring.
bout the times, I won't have to say:

Chorus:
A D
So kiss me and smile for me,
A D A Bm
tell me that you'll wait for me; hold me like you'll nev - er let me
E7 A D
go. I'm a - leav - in' on a jet plane,
A D/A 1.2. A C♯m
I don't know when I'll be back a - gain; oh, babe, I hate

Bm7
E
3.
A
to go.
2. There's so
leav - in'
D
A
D/A
on a jet plane,
I don't know when
I'll be back a - gain;
A
C♯m
Bm
oh, babe,
I hate
to
E
go.
dim.
p

LET'S SPEND THE NIGHT TOGETHER

Words and Music by
MICK JAGGER and KEITH RICHARDS

Moderately bright ♩ = 138

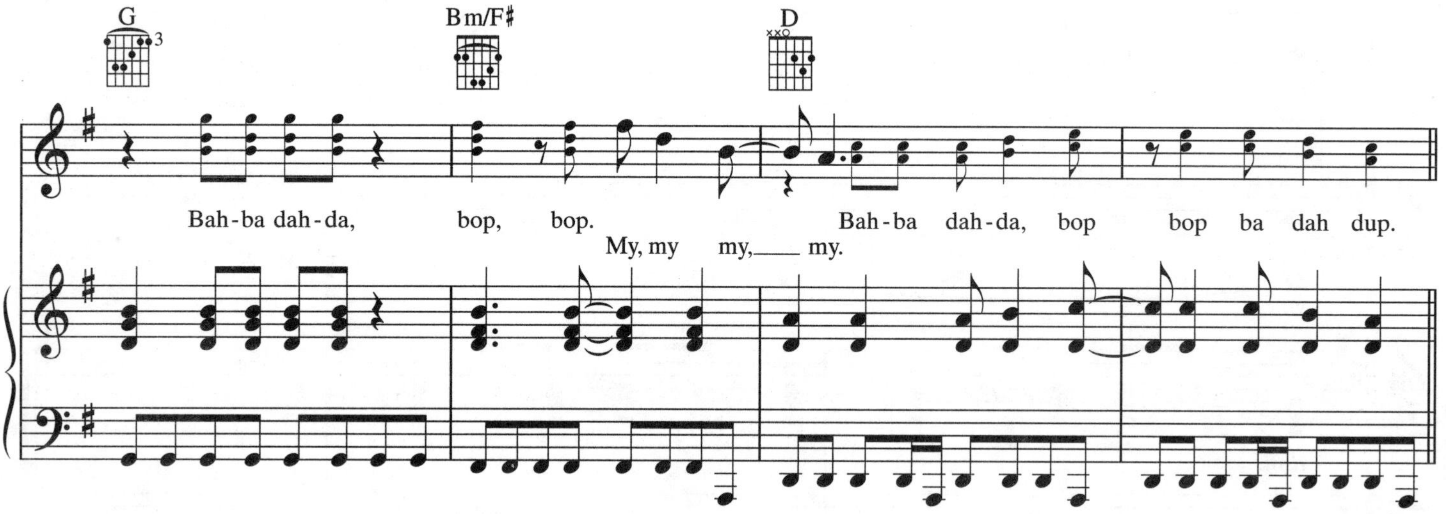

Verse:
G
Bm/F♯
D
1. Don't you wor - ry 'bout what's on your mind,_ oh, my._ Bah - ba dah - da, bop,
2. I feel so strong_ that I can't dis - guise,_ oh, my._ Let's_ spend the night
3. This does - n't hap - pen to me ev - 'ry - day,_ oh, my._ Let's_ spend the night
G
Bm/F♯
bop, ba dah dup. I'm in no hur - ry, I can take my time,_ oh,_
to - geth - er. But I just_ can't a - pol - o - gize,_ oh,_
to - geth - er. No ex - cus - es of - fered an - y - way,_ oh,_
D
C
_ my. Bah - ba dah - da, bop, bop, ba dah dup. I'm go - ing red_
_ no. Let's_ spend the night to - geth - er. Don't hang me up_
_ my. Let's_ spend the night to - geth - er. I'll sat - is - fy_

*Play Bm 2nd and 3rd time.

To Coda
now I need you more than ev - er, let's spend the night
1.
G
Bm/F♯
to - geth - er now. (Bah-ba dah-da, bop, bop.)
My, my my,
D
2.
(Bah-ba dah-da, bop bop ba dah dup.) to - geth - er.
my.
Bridge:
C
G
Let's spend the night to - geth - er. Now I need you more

C
than ev - er. Doo.
Doo.
G
C
You know I'm smil - ing, ba - by.
You need some guid -
G
ing, ba - by.
I'm just de - cid - ing, ba - by.
Now
D
I need you more than ev - er.
Let's spend the night

D.S 𝄋 al Coda
to - geth - er. Let's spend the night to - geth - er now.
𝄌 Coda
G
Bm/F♯
to - geth - er now. (Bah-ba dah-da, bop, bop.)
My, my my,
D
G
my. Let's spend the night to - geth - er.
(Bah-ba dah-da,
Repeat ad lib. and fade
Bm/F♯
D
bop, bop.)
My, my my, my. Let's spend the night to - geth - er.

MUSTANG SALLY

Words and Music by
BONNY RICE

Moderate R & B ♩ = 116

F7
Sal-ly, now ba - by,
guess you bet-ter slow your Mus-tang down.
C7
You been
G7
run-nin' all o-ver town, now,
F7
oh, I guess I have to put your flat feet on the
C7
ground.

Chorus:

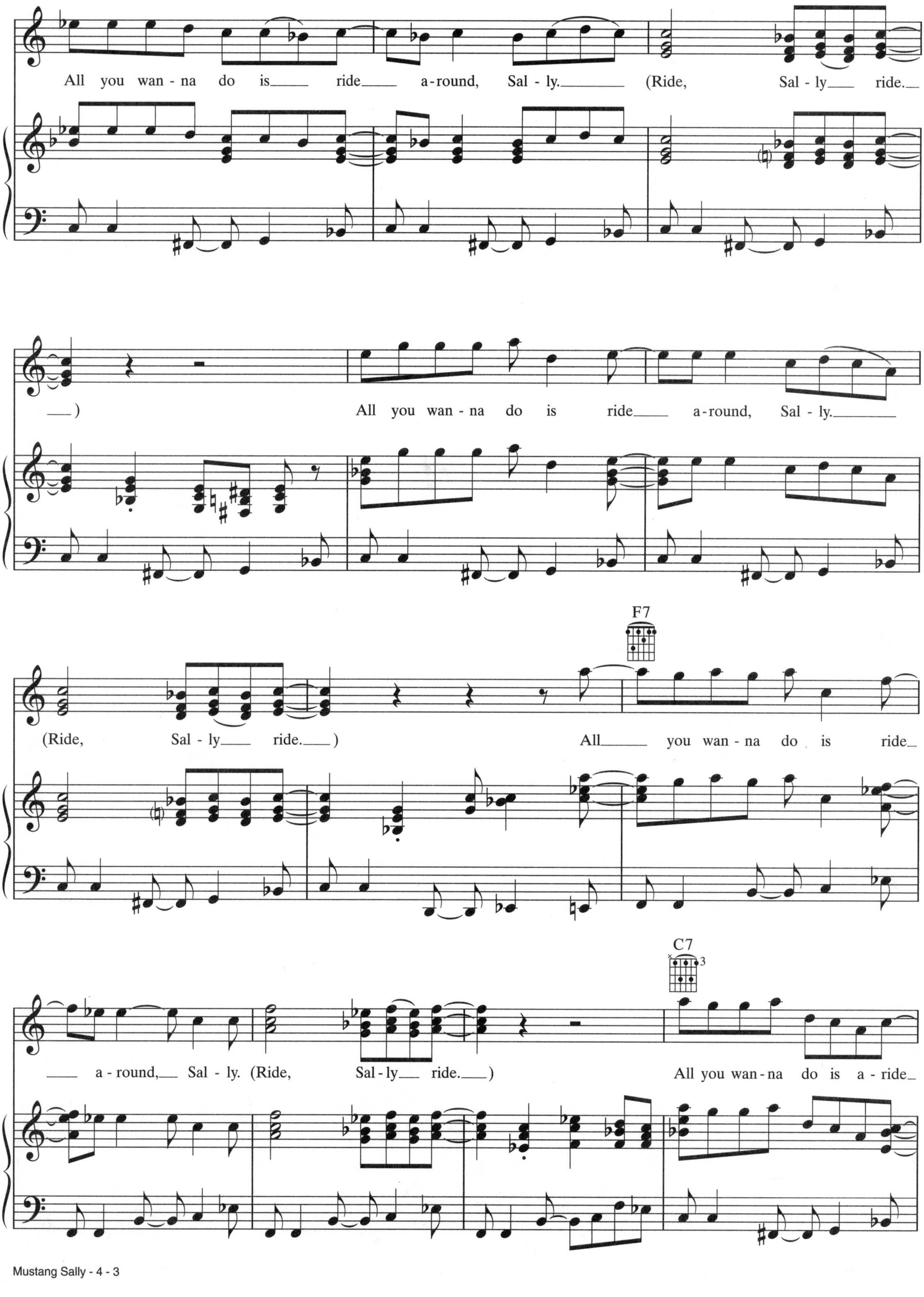

All you wan - na do is ride a - round, Sal - ly. (Ride, Sal - ly ride.
)
All you wan - na do is ride a - round, Sal - ly.
(Ride, Sal - ly ride.)
F7
All you wan - na do is ride
a - round, Sal - ly. (Ride, Sal - ly ride.)
C7
All you wan - na do is a - ride

Verse 2:
I bought you a brand-new Mustang,
About nineteen sixty-five.
Now you come around, signifying a woman,
You don't wanna let me ride.
Mustang Sally, now baby,
Guess you better slow that Mustang down.
You been runnin' all over town,
Oh, I've got to put your flat feet on the ground.
(To Chorus:)

NEEDLES AND PINS

Words and Music by
SONNY BONO and JACK NITZSCHE

Moderate rock ♩ = 120

F♯m
A
that they'd go a - way. And still, they be - gin.
F♯m
Nee - dles and pins - a. Be - cause of all my
D
E
pride, the tears I've got - ta hide.
Verse 2:
A
2. Hey! I thought I was smart. I won her heart. Did - n't think I'd

F♯m
A
do, but now, I see. She's worse to him than me. Let her go a -
F♯m
head take his love in - stead. And one day she will see just how to say,
A
F♯m
"Please," and get down on her knees.
D
Yeah, that's how it be - gins - a. She'll feel those nee - dles and

Bridge:
E
E♭
D
C♯
4
pins hurt-in' her, hurt-in' her.
Why can't I stop
C
B
and tell my-self I'm wrong? I'm wrong, so wrong!
A
A♭
4
Why can't I stand up and tell my-self I'm strong?
N.C.
D♭
4
Be-cause I saw her to-day. I saw her face. It was a face I

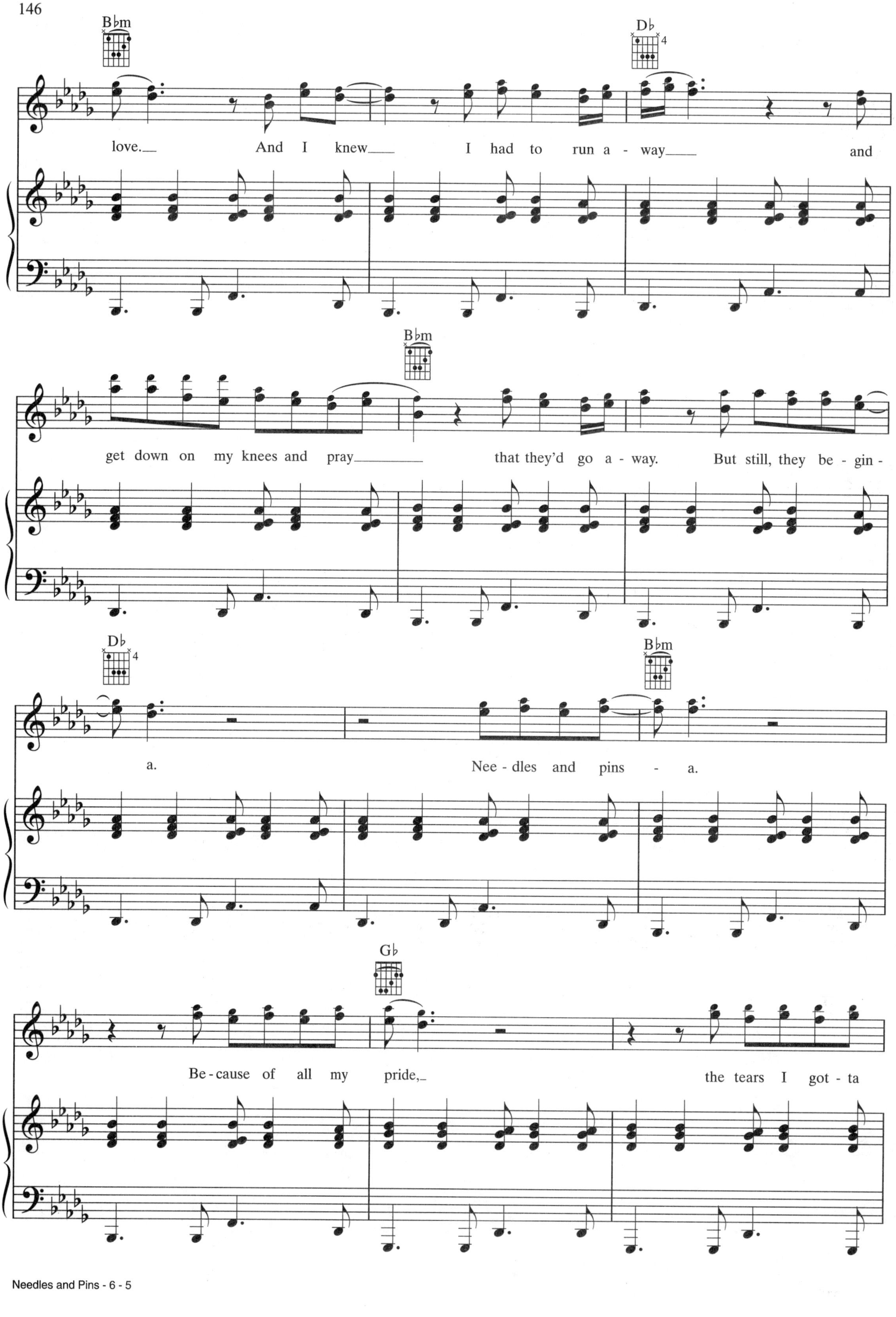
B♭m
D♭
love. And I knew I had to run a - way and
B♭m
get down on my knees and pray that they'd go a - way. But still, they be - gin -
D♭
B♭m
a. Nee - dles and pins - a.
G♭
Be - cause of all my pride, the tears I got - ta

A♭
D♭
hide.__ Oh, nee - dles and pins - a.
D♭sus D♭
D♭sus D♭
Nee - dles and pins - a. Nee - dles and pins -
D♭sus D♭
a.

PINBALL WIZARD

Words and Music by
PETER TOWNSHEND

Moderate rock ♩ = 126

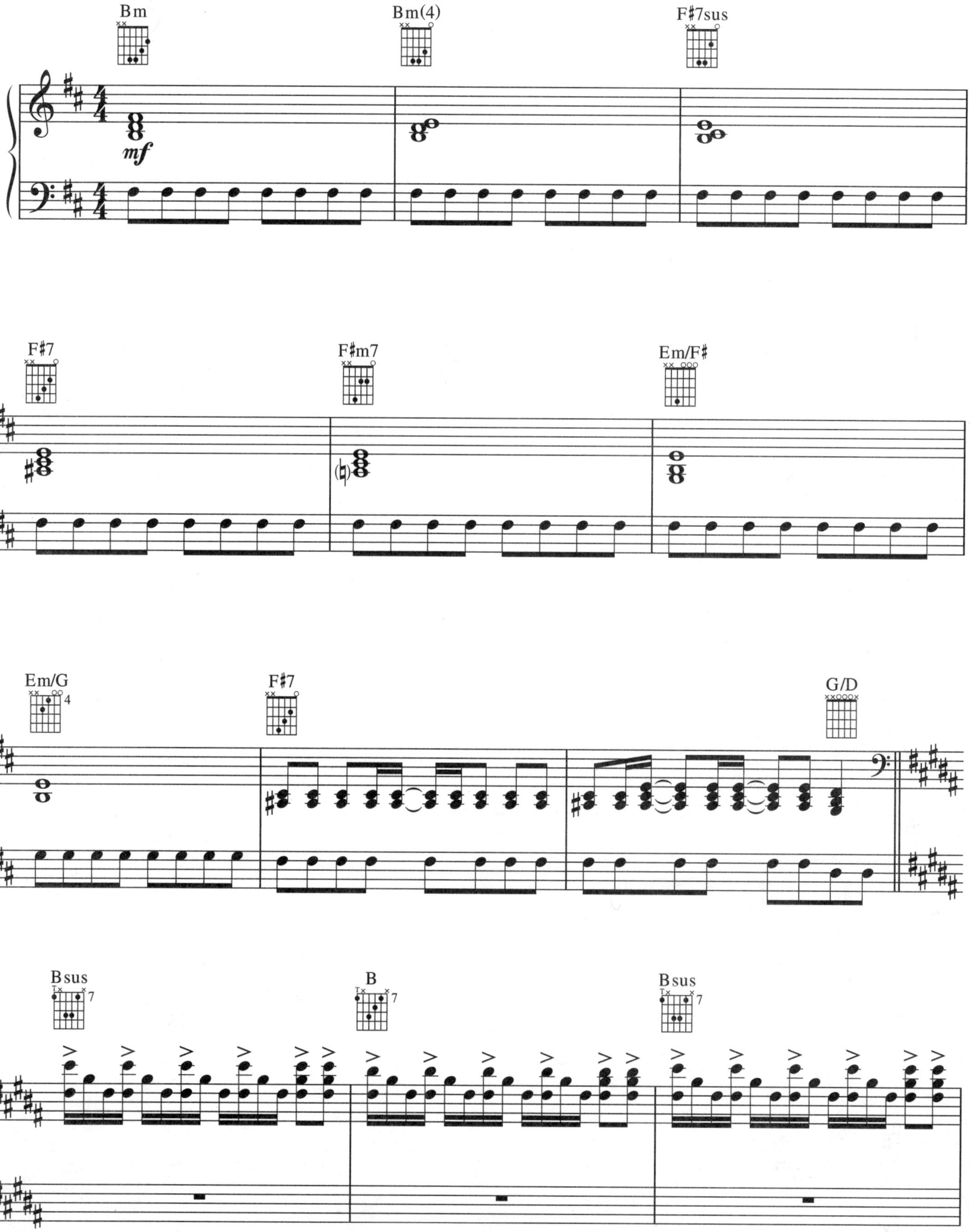

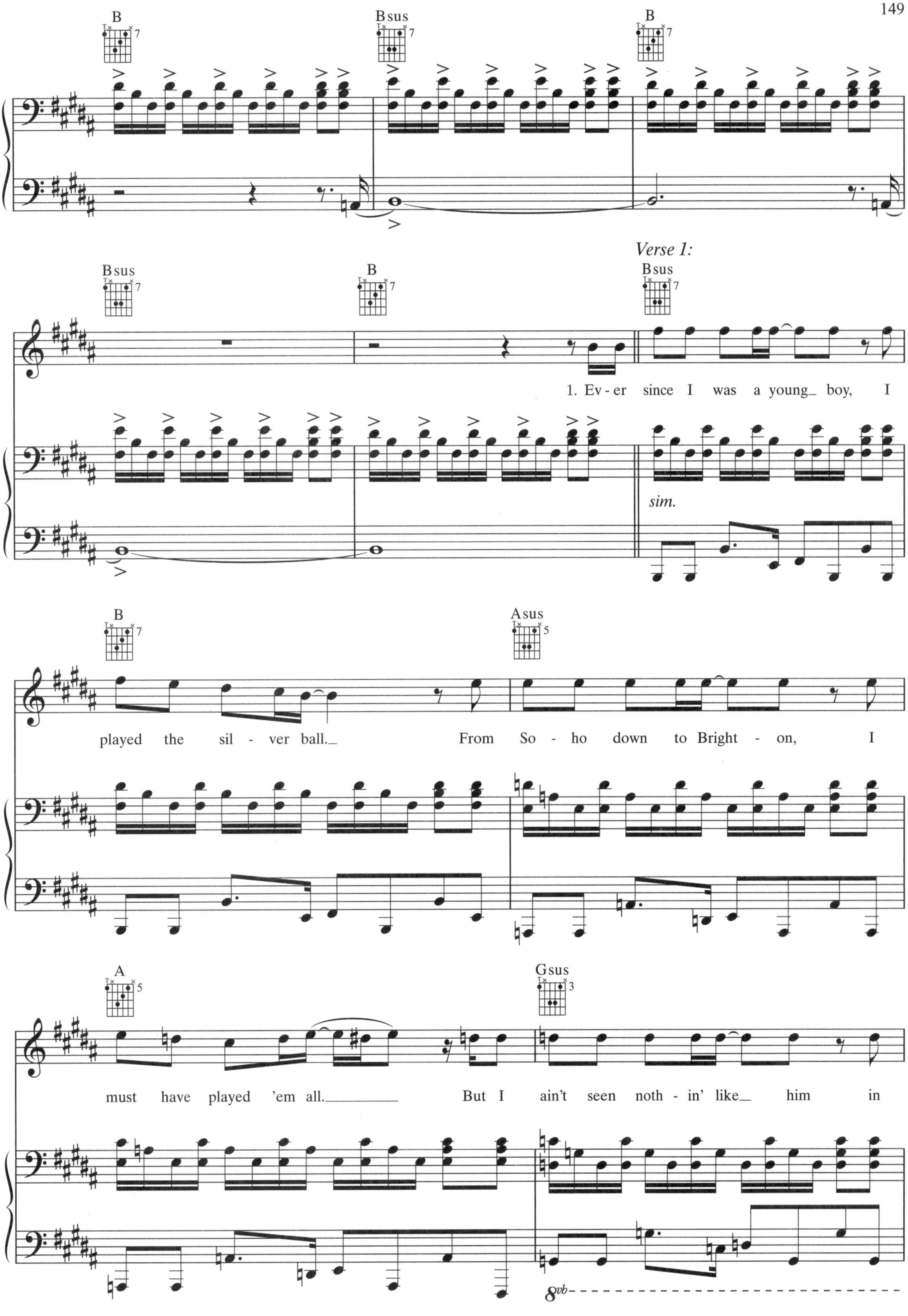
B
Bsus
B
7
Bsus
B
Verse 1:
Bsus
1. Ev - er since I was a young_ boy, I
sim.
B
Asus
5
played the sil - ver ball._ From So - ho down to Bright - on, I
A
Gsus
3
must have played 'em all.______ But I ain't seen noth - in' like_ him in
8vb

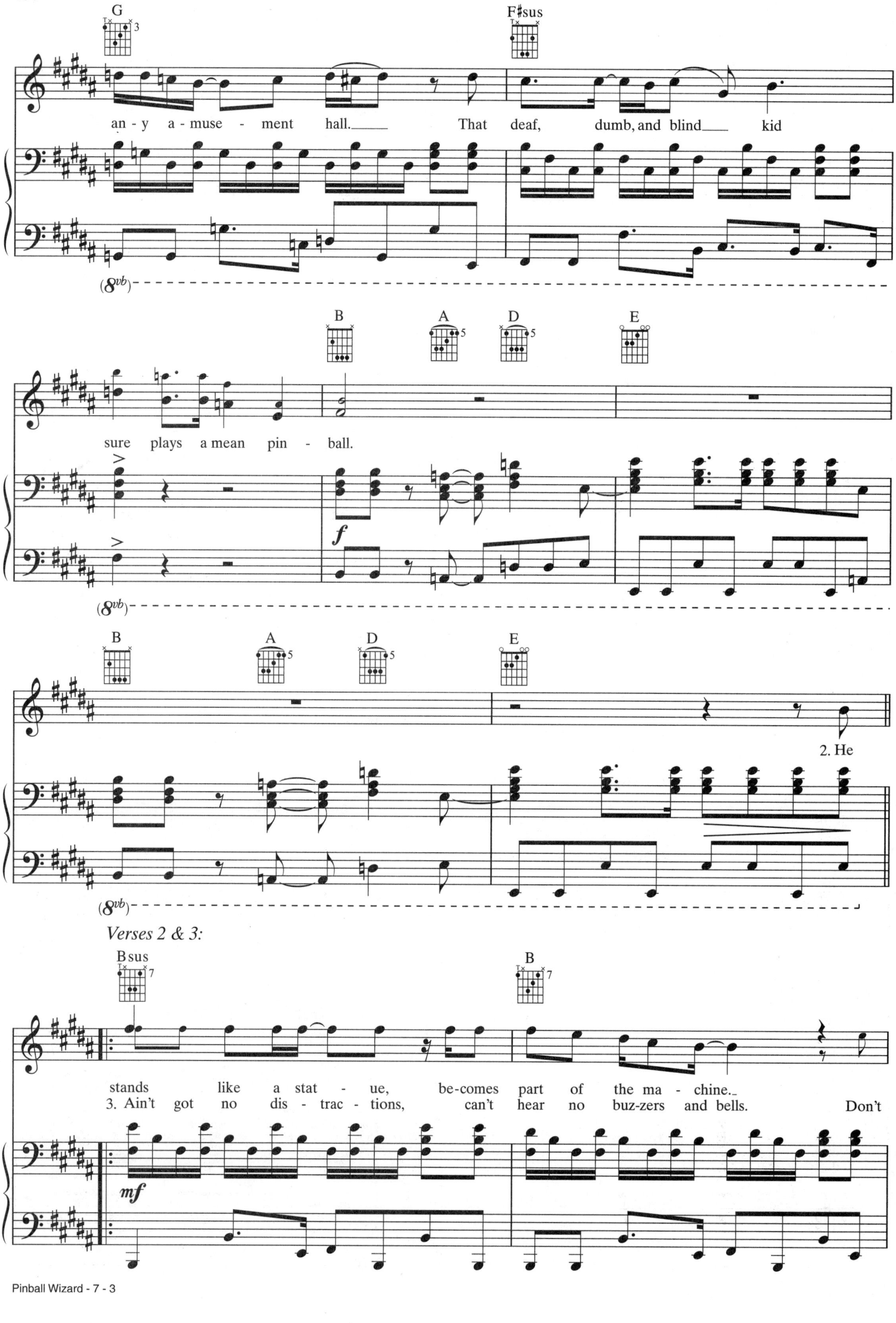
G
F♯sus
an - y a - muse - ment hall.___ That deaf, dumb, and blind___ kid
(8vb)
B
A
D
E
sure plays a mean pin - ball.
f
(8vb)
B
A
D
E
2. He
(8vb)
Verses 2 & 3:
Bsus
B
stands like a stat - ue, be - comes part of the ma - chine._
3. Ain't got no dis - trac - tions, can't hear no buz - zers and bells. Don't
mf

Asus
A
Feel - in' all ___ the bump - ers, al - ways play - in' clean. ___
see no lights a - flash - in', plays by sense of smell. ___
Gsus
G
Plays by in - tu - i - tion, the dig - it count - ers fall. ___ That
Al - ways gets the re - play, nev - er seen him fall. ___ That
8vb
F♯sus
B
A
D
deaf, dumb, _ and blind ___ kid sure plays a mean pin - ball.
deaf, dumb, _ and blind ___ kid sure plays a mean pin - ball.
f
(8vb)
E
B
A
D
E
He's a
I
(8vb)

Chorus:
F♯ B E F♯ B E F♯ B
pin - ball wiz - ard, there has to be a twist. A pin - ball wiz-ard's got
thought I was the Bal - ly ta - ble king, but I just hand - ed my
G D Dsus 1. D
such a sup - ple wrist.
pin - ball crown to him.
C2 G/B D C2 G/B D C2 G/B
How do you think he does it?
(I don't know.)
What makes him so
mf
D 2. D
good?

Dsus
D
Dsus
mf
sim.
D
Dsus
D
Dsus
D
4. E - ven
Verse 4:
Dsus
D
on my fa - v'rite ta - ble, he can beat my best. His di -

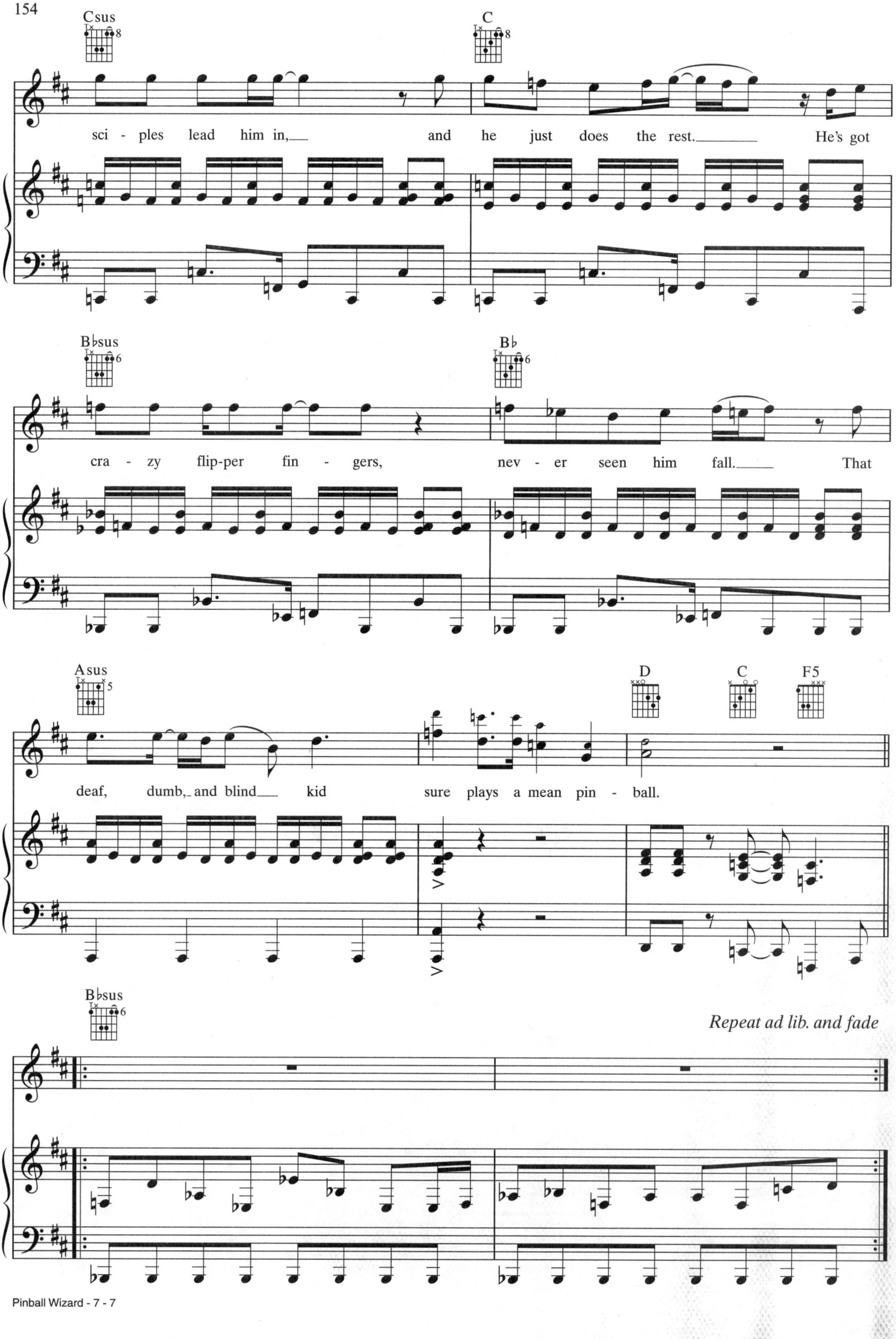
Csus
C
sci - ples lead him in, and he just does the rest. He's got
B♭sus
B♭
cra - zy flip-per fin - gers, nev - er seen him fall. That
Asus
D
C
F5
deaf, dumb, and blind kid sure plays a mean pin - ball.
B♭sus
Repeat ad lib. and fade

PUT A LITTLE LOVE IN YOUR HEART

Words and Music by
JIMMY HOLIDAY, RANDY MYERS
and JACKIE DE SHANNON

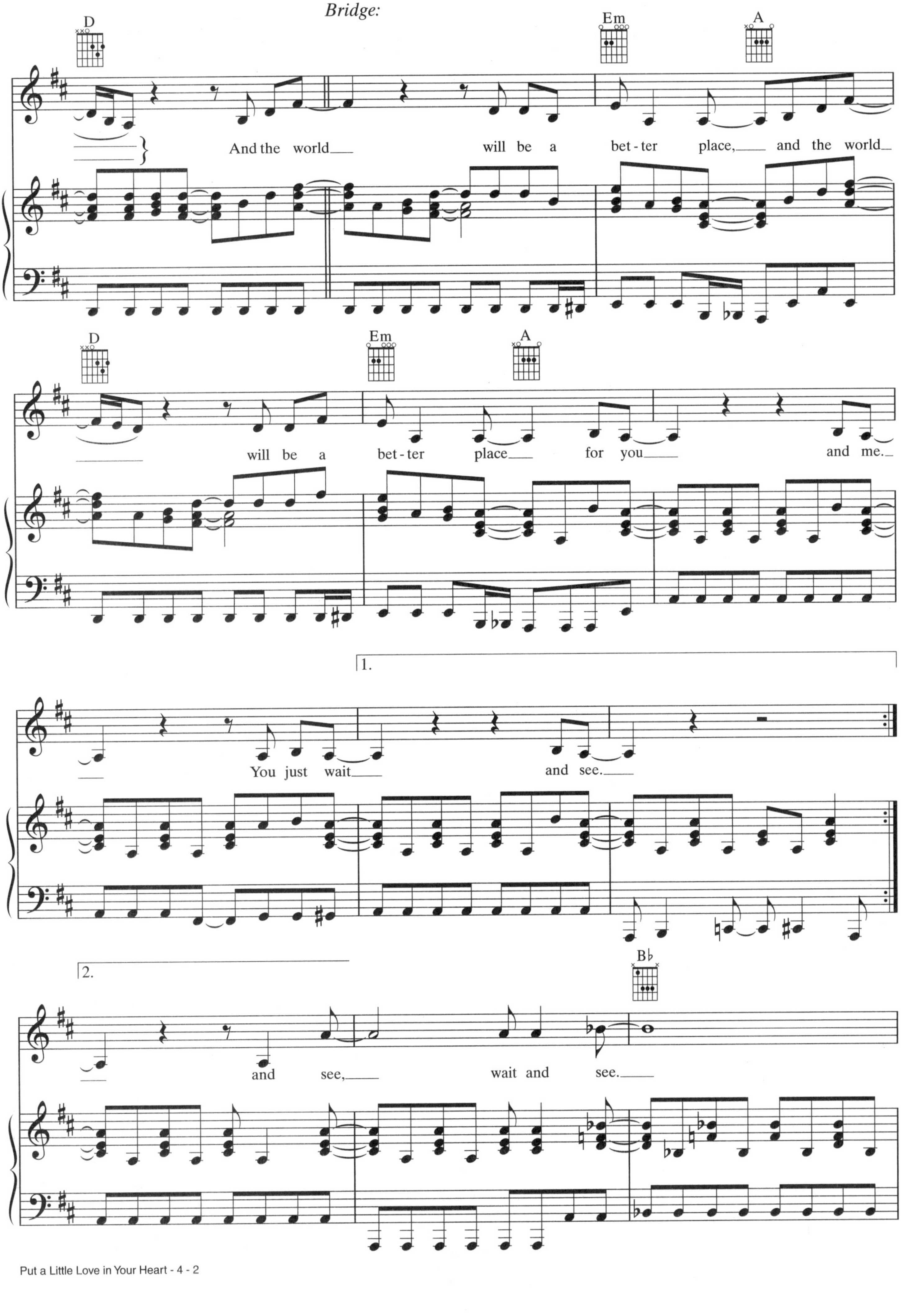
Bridge:
D
Em
A
And the world will be a bet-ter place, and the world
D
Em
A
will be a bet-ter place for you and me.
1.
You just wait and see.
2.
B♭
and see, wait and see.

Verse 3:
B♭7
E♭
3. Take a good look_ a-round, and if you're look-in' down,
A♭
E♭
put a lit-tle love_ in your heart.____ I hope when you_ de-cide
A♭
E♭
kind-ness will be your guide,_ put a lit-tle love_ in your heart.____ And the world_
Bridge:
Fm
B♭
E♭
__ (and the world) will be a bet-ter place,_ and the world__ (and the world) will be a

Fm
B♭
bet - ter place for you (for you) and me. (and me) You just wait
(just wait) and see.
A♭
E♭
Put a lit - tle love in your heart.
A♭
E♭
Put a lit - tle love in your heart.
A♭
Put a lit - tle love in your heart.
E♭
A♭
E♭
Repeat ad lib. and fade
Put a lit - tle love in your heart.

ROSES ARE RED (MY LOVE)

Words and Music by
AL BYRON and PAUL EVANS

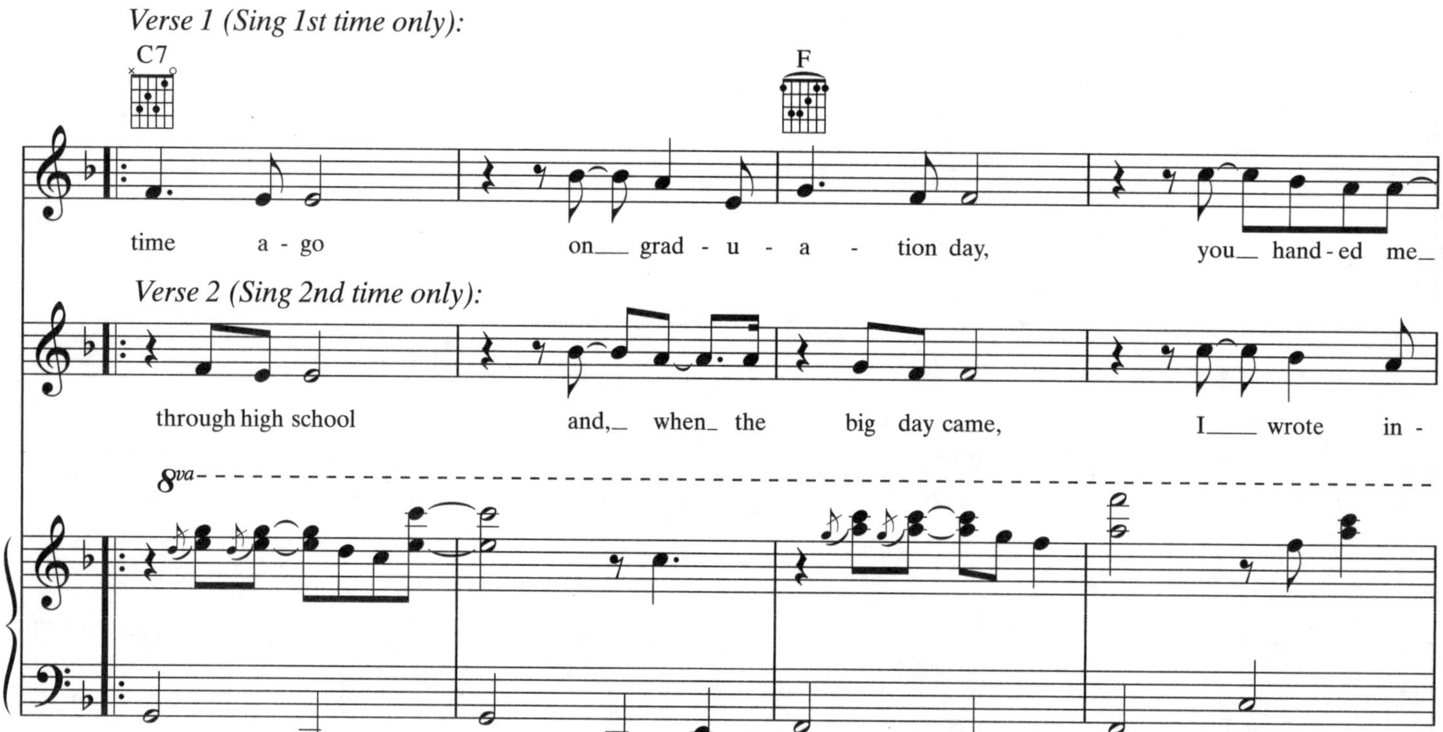

B♭
C7
F
C7/E
F/E♭
your book.
I signed this way, "Ros - es are
to your book next to my name, "Ros - es are
(8va)
Chorus:
B♭
F
Dm
red, my love.
Vio-lets are blue.
Su - gar is
8va
3
B♭
C7
1.
F
sweet, my love, but not as sweet as you."
(8va)

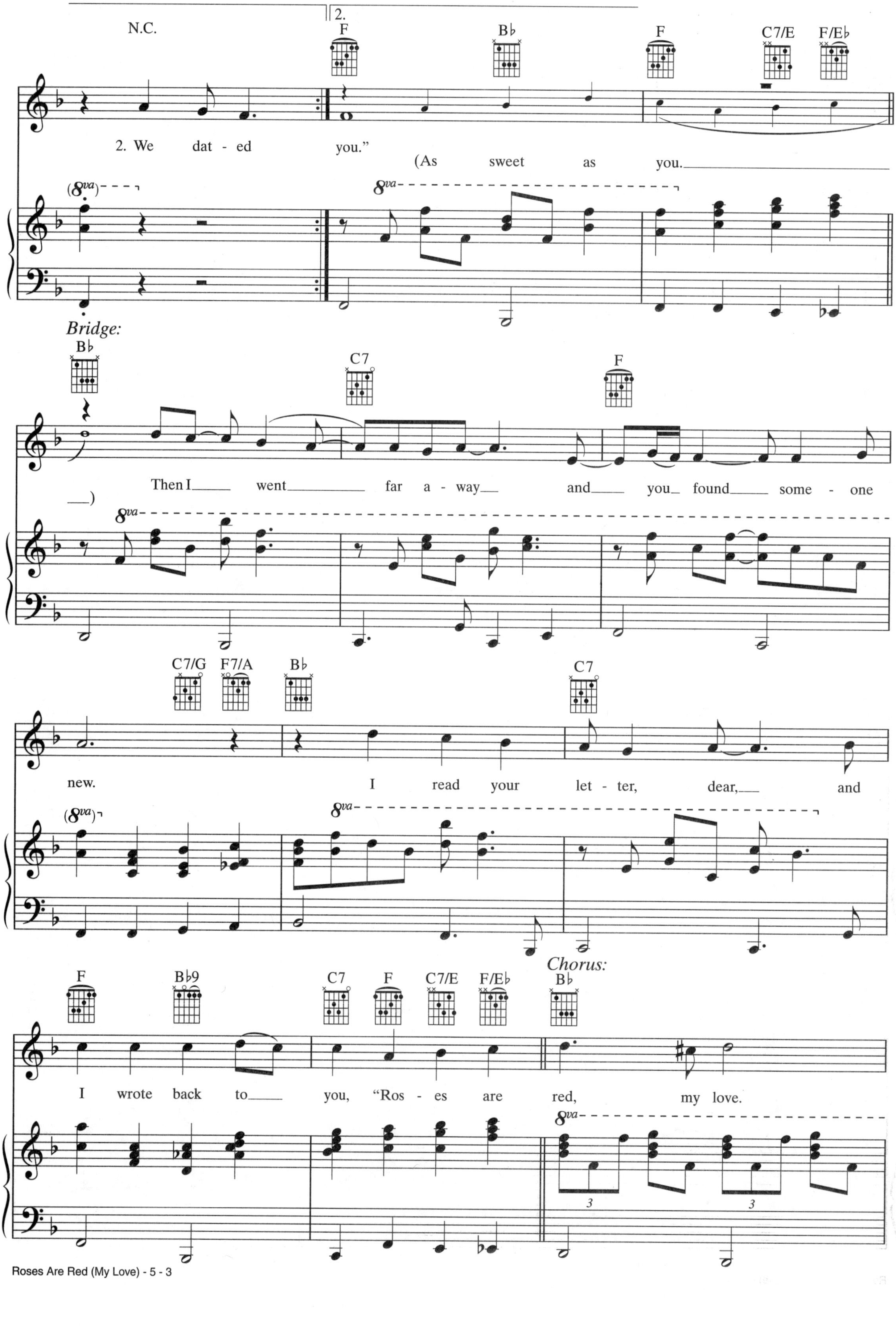
N.C.
2.
F Bb F C7/E F/Eb
2. We dat - ed you."
(As sweet as you.
Bridge:
Bb C7 F
Then I went far a - way and you found some - one
)
C7/G F7/A Bb C7
new. I read your let - ter, dear, and
F Bb9 C7 F C7/E F/Eb
Chorus:
Bb
I wrote back to you, "Ros - es are red, my love.
8va

F
Dm
Vio - lets are blue.
Su - gar is
B♭
C7
F
C7sus
sweet, my love. Good luck! May God bless You!
(May God bless
N.C.
Verse 3:
C7
3. Is that your lit - tle girl?
She looks
you!)
F
B♭
a lot like you. Some day, some boy will write

Chorus:
C7 F C7/E F/E♭ B♭
in her book too, "Ros - es are red, my love.
F Dm
Vio - lets are blue. Su - gar is
B♭ C7 F B♭ F/A Gm7 F
sweet, my love, but not as sweet as you.
(Ros - es are red.)
rit.

(I CAN'T GET NO) SATISFACTION

Words and Music by
MICK JAGGER and KEITH RICHARDS

Moderate rock ♩ = 136

E
A
I can't get no
1.2. sat - is -
3. girl re -
E
B
fac - tion,
ac - tion,
'cause I try
and I try
and I try
E
A
E
D
and I try.
I can't get no,
A
E
D
A
I can't get no...
1.2.3. When I'm

Verse:
E D A E D
driv - in' in my car and the man comes on the ra -
2.3. See additional lyrics
A E D A
di - o; he's tell - in' me more and more a - bout some
E D A E D
use - less in - for - ma - tion, sup - posed to fire my i - mag - i - na -
A E D A
tion. I can't get no, oh, no, no,

E N.C. E D
no. Hey, hey, hey,
A E D 1.2. A
that's what I say.
3. A E D A
I can't get no, I can't
E D A E D
get no, I can't get no,

Verse 2:
When I'm watchin' my TV,
And a man comes on and tells me
How white my shirts can be,
But he can't be a man 'cause he doesn't smoke
The same cigarettes as me.
I can't get no, oh, no, no, no.
Hey, hey, hey, that's what I say.
(To Chorus:)

Verse 3:
When I'm ridin' 'round the world,
And I'm doin' this and I'm signin' that,
And I'm tryin' to make some girl
Who tells me, baby, better come back maybe next week,
'Cause you see I'm on a losin' streak.
I can't get no, oh, no, no, no.
Hey, hey, hey, that's what I say.
I can't get no...

SCARBOROUGH FAIR/CANTICLE

Arrangement and original counter melody by
PAUL SIMON and ARTHUR GARFUNKEL

*Harmony notes sung last time only.

A13sus
A2
E13sus
E2
thyme.
Re -
C
G/B
Am7
G
G
D/F♯
Em7
D
mem - ber me to one who lives there.
Am
Em
She once was a true love of
A13sus
E13sus
To Coda
mine.

Verse 2:

A13sus A2 G A13sus
E13sus E2 D E13sus
2. Tell her to make me a cam - bric shirt.
On the side of a hill in the
A2 C Am C D
E2 G Em G A
Pars - ley, sage, rose - mar - y, and
deep for - est green,
A13sus A2 A13sus A2
E13sus E2 E13sus E2
thyme. With -
trac - ing of spar - row on snow - crest - ed brown

C G/B Am7 G
G D/F♯ Em7 D
out no seams nor nee - dle - work,
blan - kets and bed - clothes, the
Am G Am G Am G
Em D Em D Em D
then she'll be a true love of
child of the moun - tain
A13sus A2 A13sus A2
E13sus E2 E13sus E2
mine.
sleeps un - a - ware of the clar - i - on call.

Verse 3:
A13sus A2 G A13sus
E13sus E2 D E13sus
3. Tell her to find me an a - cre of land.
On the side of a hill, a
A2 C Am C D
E2 G Em G A
Pars - ley, sage, rose - mar - y, and
sprink - ling of leaves.
A13sus A2 A13sus A2
E13sus E2 E13sus E2
thyme. With -
Wash - es the grave with sil - ver - y tears.

C
G
G/B
D/F#
Am7
Em7
G
D
tween the salt - wa - ter and the sea strands.
A sol - dier cleans and
Am
Em
G
D
Am
Em
G
D
Am
Em
G
D
Then she'll be a true love of
pol - ish - es a gun.
A13sus
E13sus
A2
E2
A13sus
E13sus
A2
E2
mine.

Verse 4:
A13sus
E13sus
A2
E2
G
D
A13sus
E13sus
4. Tell her to reap it in a sickle of leath - er.
War bel - lows blaz - ing in
A2
E2
C
G
Am
Em
C
G
D
A
Par - sley, sage, rose - mar - y, and
scar - let bat - tal - lions.
A13sus
E13sus
A2
E2
A13sus
E13sus
A2
E2
thyme.
And
Gen - er - als or - der their sol - diers to kill.

C G/B Am7 G
G D/F♯ Em7 D
gath - er it all in a bunch of heath - er.
And to fight for a cause they've
Am G Am G Am G
Em D Em D Em D
Then she'll be a true love of
long a - go for - got - ten.
A13sus A2 A13sus A2
E13sus E2 E13sus E2
D.S 𝄋 al Coda
mine.
Coda
A13sus
E13sus

STAND BY YOUR MAN

Words and Music by
TAMMY WYNETTE and BILLY SHERRILL

Moderately slow country ♩ = 54

A
D/F♯
A/E
E
mp
(with pedal)
Verse:
A
E
Some-times it's hard to be a wom-an,
Bm7
E7
A
giv-ing all you love to just one man.

D
A
You'll have bad times and he'll have good times,
B7
E7
do-in' things that you don't un-der-stand.
A
E
But if you love him, you'll for-give him,
Bm7
E7
A
e-ven though he's hard to un-der-stand.

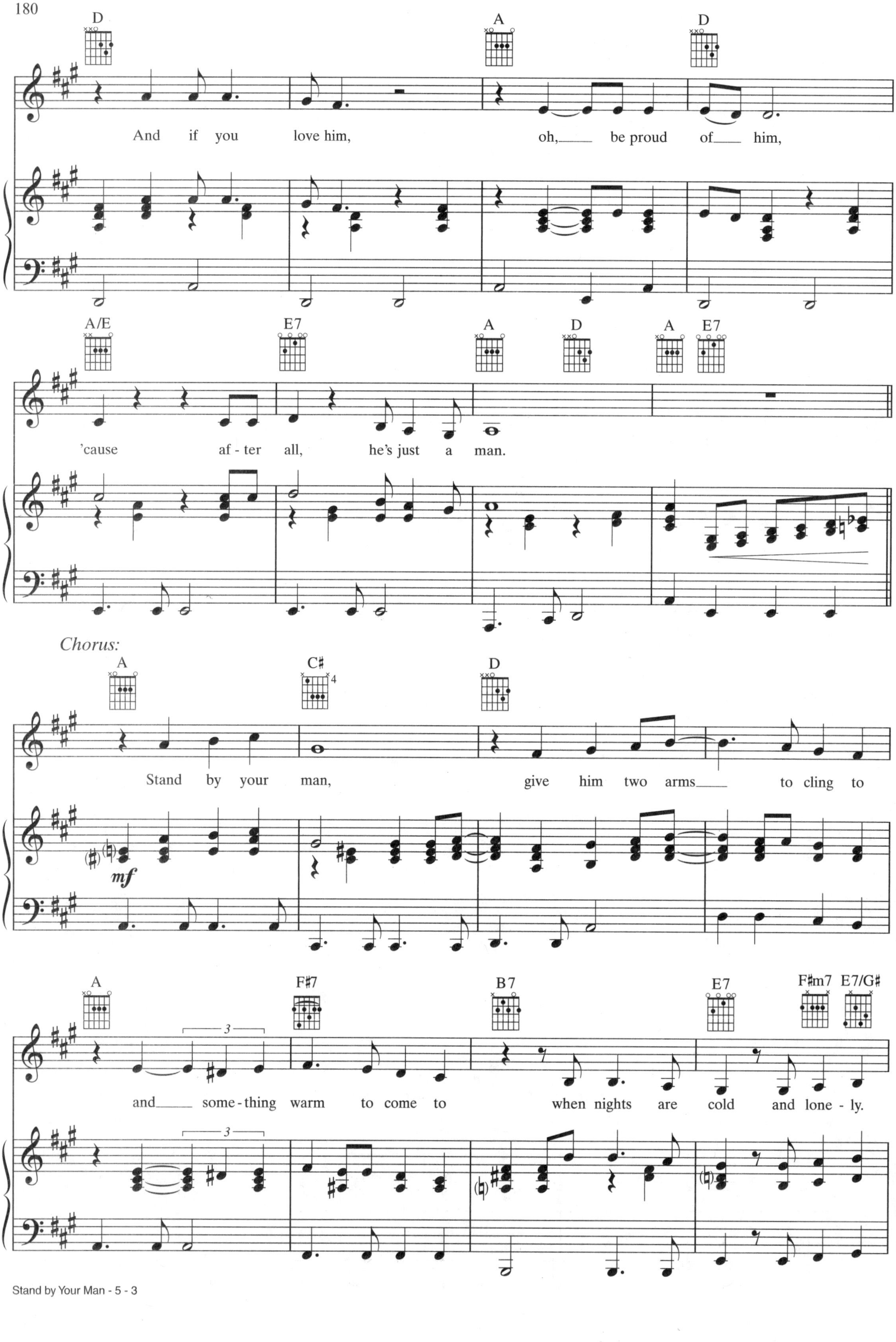
D
A
D
And if you love him,
oh,___ be proud of___ him,
A/E
E7
A
D
A
E7
'cause af - ter all, he's just a man.
Chorus:
A
C♯
4
D
Stand by your man,
give him two arms___ to cling to
mf
A
F♯7
B7
E7
F♯m7
E7/G♯
3
and___ some-thing warm to come to
when nights are cold and lone - ly.

A
C♯
D
Stand by your man, and show the world___ you love him,
A
E
C♯7
F♯
keep giv - in' all the love you can.
dim.
D
E
A
D
A
E7
Stand by your___ man._
mp
A
C♯
D
Stand by your man, and show the world_
mf

A
E
you love him, keep giv - in' all the love you can.
C♯7
F♯7
D
E7
Stand by your
A
D/F♯
A/E
Bm
E7
A
man.
rit.

A SUMMER SONG

Words and Music by
CLIVE METCALF, KEITH NOBLE
and DAVID STUART

Moderately ♩ = 122

A C♯m D E A C♯m D E
mf
Verse 1:
A C♯m D E A C♯m
1. Trees sway-ing in the sum-mer breeze,
D E A C♯m D E
show-ing off their sil - ver leaves as we walked

A C♯m D E A C♯m
by. Soft kiss - es on a sum - mer's day
D E A C♯m D E
laugh - ing all our cares a - way, just you and
A C♯m D E
Verse 2:
A C♯m
I
2. Sweet
D E A C♯m D E
sleep - y warmth of sum - mer nights, gaz - ing at the

A C♯m D E A C
dis - tant lights__ in the star - ry sky.
Bridge:
D A D E
They say all all good things must
A F♯m D
end some day. Au - tumn
E F♯m
leaves must__ fall. But

A
C♯7
F♯m
don't you know that it hurts me so___ to say good - bye to
C♯m
Bm
F♯m
E
you?___ Wish you did - n't have to go,
F♯m
E
Verses 3 & 4:
A
C♯m
no, no, no no.___ 3.4. And when the rain___
D
E
A
C♯m
D
E
___ beats a - gainst my win - dow pane,_ I'll think of sum - mer

To Coda
A
C♯m
D
E
A
C♯m
days a - gain
and dream of
you.
D.S 𝄋 al Coda
D
E
A
C
D
A
3
Coda
A
C♯m
D
E
you,
and dream of
A
C♯m
D
E
F♯
you.
rit.

A TASTE OF HONEY

Words by
RIC MARLOW

Music by
BOBBY SCOTT

B♭9
Fm
Fm(maj7)
Fm7
B♭9
Fm
A♭
Gm
N.C.
D♭
Fm
1.
N.C.
2.3.
N.C.

Fm7
B♭9
Fm7
(2nd time inst. solo ad lib.…
B♭9
Slowly & freely
D♭
Cm
…end solo)
3
rit.
r.h.
mp
1.
Tempo I
N.C.
D.S.𝄋
drums
mf
2.
Tempo I
N.C.
Fm
mf

F♯m
F♯m
F♯m(maj7)
F♯m7
B9
F♯m
F♯m(maj7)
F♯m7
B9
F♯m

A
G♯m
4
3
A
G♯m
4
A
G♯m
4
N.C.
8va
8va

TELL HER NO

Words and Music by
ROD ARGENT

F♯m
B6
— you with her charms, —
— you with her charms, —
ber she said that to me. —
Tell her
cresc.
Chorus:
C♯m
4
E
no, no, no, no, no, no, no, no, no, no, no, no, no, no, no, no, no,
mf
To Coda
1.
C♯m
4
Emaj7
F♯m7
B
no, no, no, no, no. Don't hurt me, now, — for her love — be - longs — to —
(3.) Don't leave me now, — for her love —
2.
F♯m7
B
Emaj7
— be - longs — to — me.
cresc.

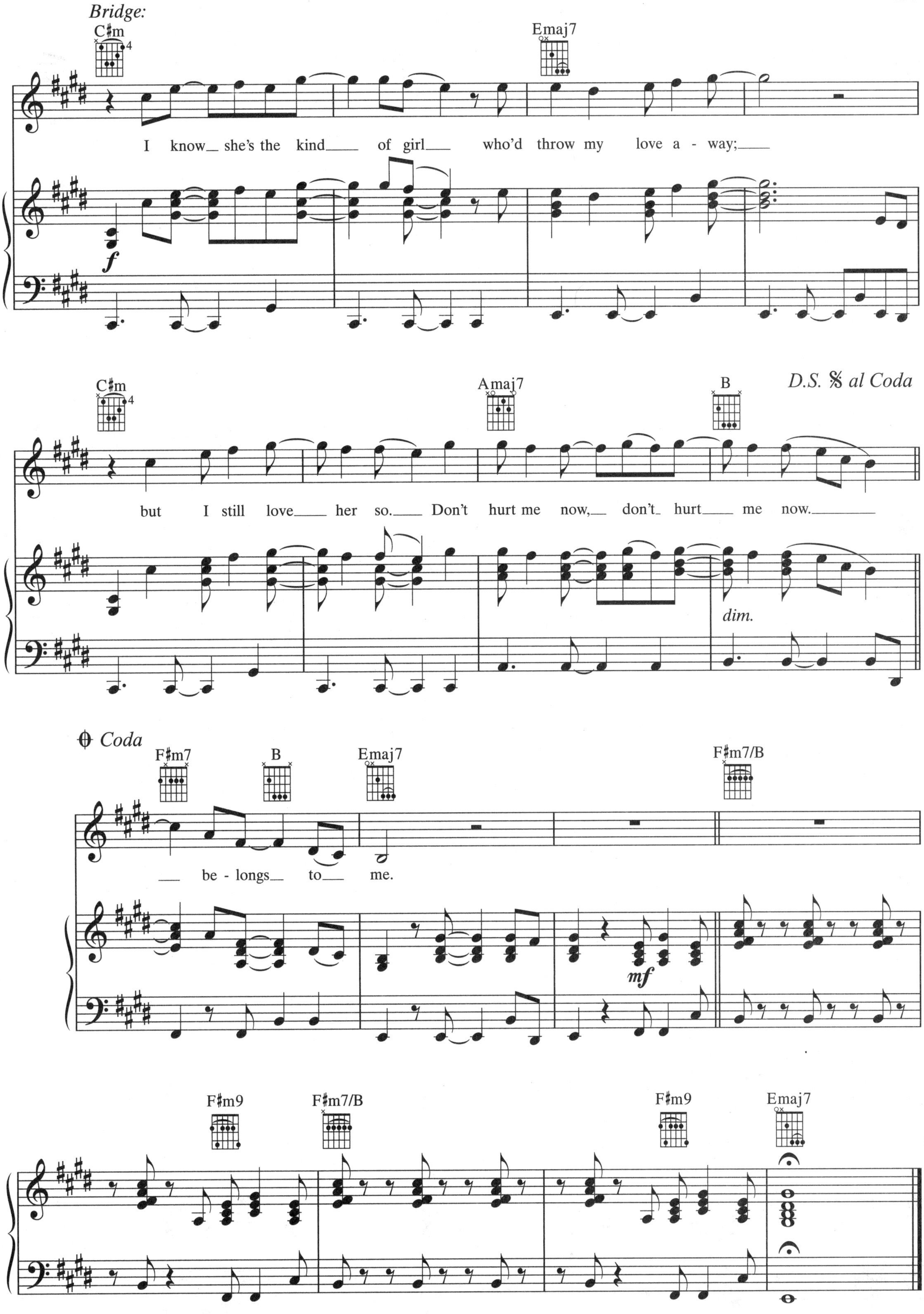
Bridge:
C♯m
Emaj7
I know_ she's the kind___ of girl___ who'd throw my love a - way;___
f
C♯m
Amaj7
B
D.S. 𝄋 al Coda
but I still love___ her so.___ Don't hurt me now,__ don't_ hurt___ me now.______
dim.
𝄌 Coda
F♯m7
B
Emaj7
F♯m7/B
__ be - longs__ to__ me.
mf
F♯m9
F♯m7/B
F♯m9
Emaj7

TIME OF THE SEASON

Words and Music by
ROD ARGENT

Moderate rock ♩ = 116

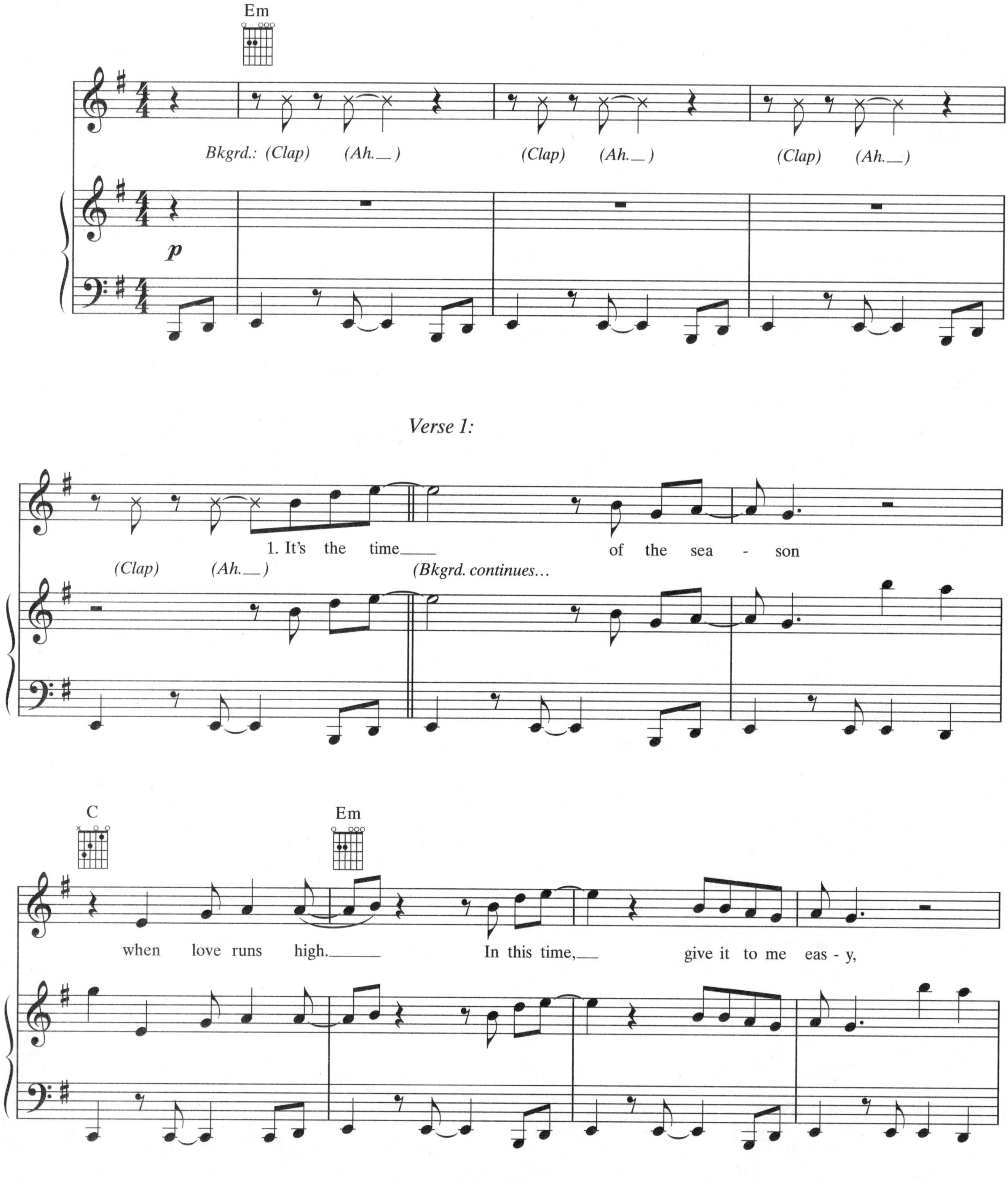

C
Em
G
and let me try___ with pleas-ured hands___ to take you in the
...end Bkgrd.)
cresc.
mf
Em
G
Em
D(9)
C
sun to prom-ised lands,___ to show you ev-'ry one.___ It's the time___
f
G
Am7
E
of the sea - son for lov - ing.
Em
2. What's your name?
Bkgrd.: (Clap) (Ah.__) (Clap) (Ah.__) (Clap) (Ah.__) (Clap) (Ah.__)

Verses 2 & 3:
Em
C
(3.) (Bkgrd. continues... Who's your dad-dy? Is he rich like me?
(What's your name? Who's your dad-dy? He rich?
Em
Has he tak - en an - y time
Has he tak - en an - y time to
C
Em
G
to show you what you need to live?
show) ...end Bkgrd.)
Tell it to me
cresc.
mf
Em
G
Em
D(9)
C
slow - ly; tell you why, I real - ly want to know. It's the time
f

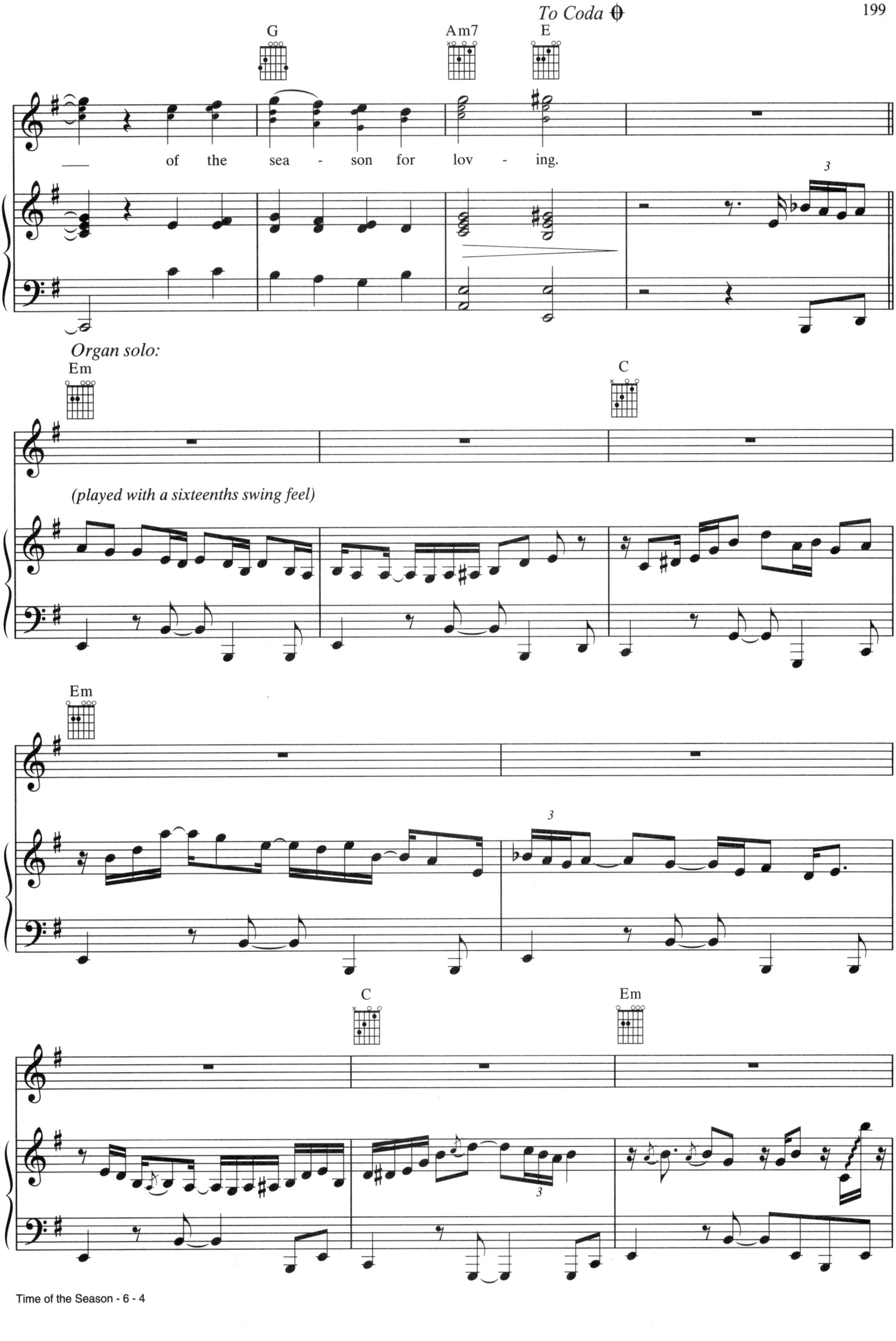
To Coda
G
Am7
E
of the sea - son for lov - ing.
3
Organ solo:
Em
C
(played with a sixteenths swing feel)
Em
3
C
Em
3

G
Em
G
Em
C
Bm
Am7
E
Em
Bkgrd.: (Clap)
(Ah.___)
(end solo)
D.S 𝄋 al Coda
(Clap)
(Ah.__)
(Clap)
(Ah.__)
(Clap)
(Ah.__)
3. What's your name?_

Coda
Organ solo:
Em
mf
C
Em
3
3
3
Repeat ad lib. and fade
C
Em

TWISTIN' THE NIGHT AWAY

Words and Music by
SAM COOKE

Moderate rock swing ♩ = 144
A
G
A
D/A
A
D/A
A
G
A
mf
Verse:
1. Let me tell you 'bout a place
2. Here's a man in eve - ning clothes.
3. See additional lyrics
F♯m
some - where up in New York way
How he got here I don't know, but

D
E7
where the peo-ple are so gay, twist - in' the night a - way.
man, you ought to see him go, twist - in' the night a - way.
A
8va
Here they have a lot of fun,
He's danc - ing with the chick in slacks,
F♯m
D
put - tin' trou - ble on the run. Man, you'll find the
she's mov - ing up and back. Oh man, there ain't
E7
A
old and young twist - in' the night a way.
noth - ing like twist - in' the night a - way.
They're twist -

Chorus:
in', twist - ing. Ev - ry - bod - y's feel - ing great. They're twist -
D
in', twist - ing. They're twist - in' the night a - way.
1.
E7
A
2.3.
E7
A
A
in' the night. (Let's twist a while!). (Lean up, lean
(Sax. solo ad lib....
F♯m
D
back, lean up, lean

Verse 3:
Here's a fellow in blue jeans
Dancing with an older queen
Whose dolled up in-a diamond rings
And twisting the night away.
Man, you oughta see her go,
Twistin' to the rock and roll.
Here you'll find the young and old
Twistin' the night away.
(To Chorus:)

WHAT'S NEW PUSSYCAT?

Words by
HAL DAVID

Music by
BURT BACHARACH

Bright waltz ♩ = 188

Chorus:

Verse:
A
Cmaj7
1. Pus - sy - cat, Pus - sy - cat, I've got flow - ers and
2. Pus - sy - cat, Pus - sy - cat, you're so thrill - ing and
3. Pus - sy - cat, Pus - sy - cat, you're de - li - cious and,
mf
B♭
lots of hours to spend with you.
I'm so will - ing to care for you.
if my wish - es can all come true,
So go and pow - der your cute lit - tle pus - sy - cat nose.
So go and make up your big lit - tle pus - sy - cat eyes.
I'll soon be kiss - ing your sweet lit - tle pus - sy - cat lips.
A
Pus - sy - cat, Pus - sy - cat,
Pus - sy - cat, Pus - sy - cat,
Pus - sy - cat, Pus - sy - cat,

D7
C♯m7
Bm7
E13
I love you. Yes, I
I love you. Yes, I
I love you. Yes, I
C♯m7
F♯m7
To Coda
Bm7
E7
do.
do.
do.
You and your pus - sy - cat nose.
You and your pus - sy - cat eyes.
Chorus:
A
D
G6
What's new, Pus - sy - cat?
f
A13
D
G6
Whoa.
What's new, Pus - sy - cat?

A13
D
Whoa, oh.
1.
2.
E7
D.S 𝄋 al Coda
𝄌 Coda
Bm7
E7
A
You and your pus - sy - cat lips.
(Whoa.)
You and your pus - sy - cat eyes.
(Whoa.)
You and your pus - sy - cat nose.
poco rit.

WOODSTOCK

Gtr. tuned down 1/2 step:
⑥ = E♭ ③ = G♭
⑤ = A♭ ② = B♭
④ = D♭ ① = E♭

Words and Music by
JONI MITCHELL

Moderately slow ♩ = 108

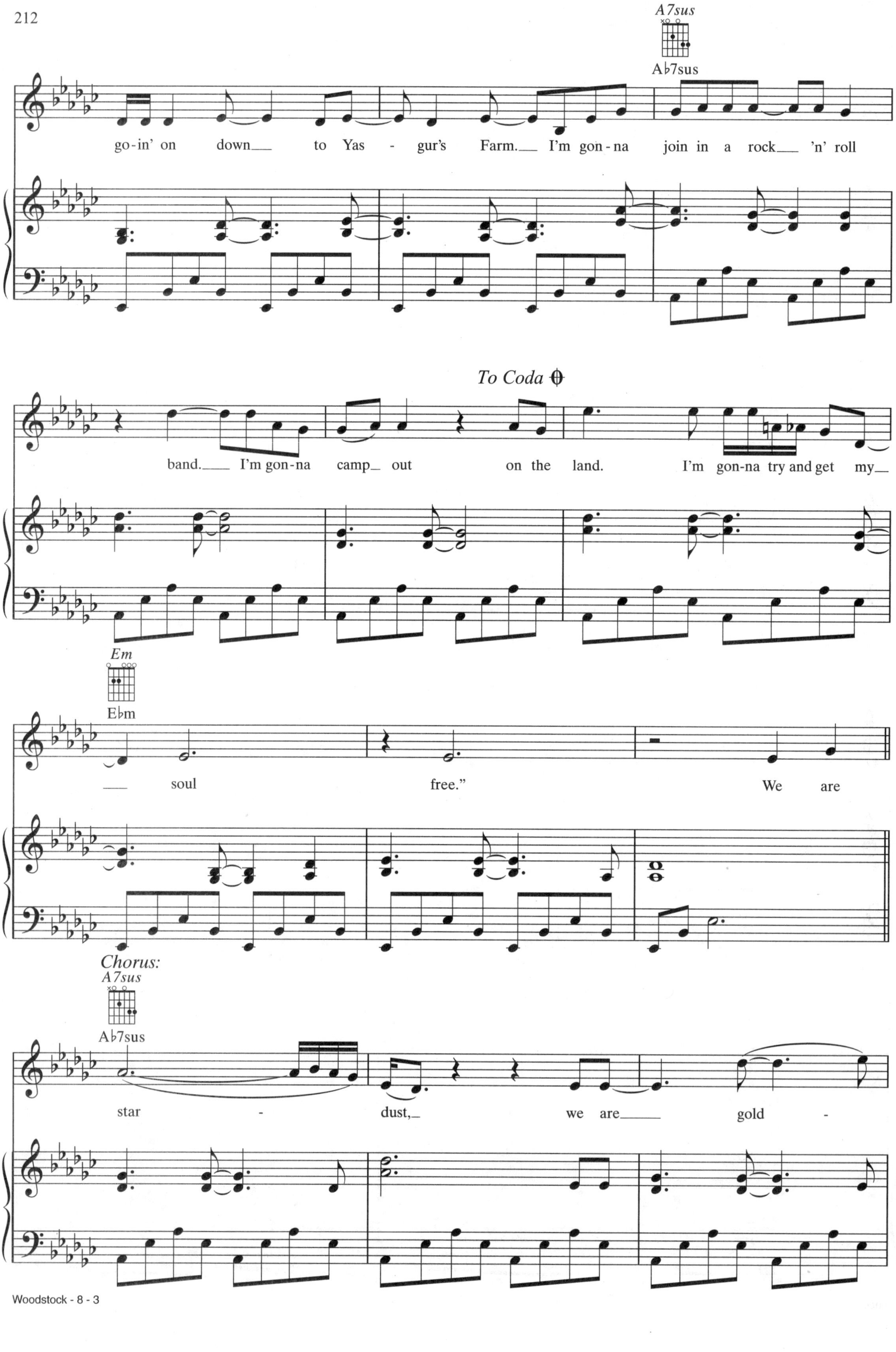
A7sus
Ab7sus
go-in' on down___ to Yas - gur's Farm.___ I'm gon-na join in a rock___ 'n' roll
To Coda
band.___ I'm gon-na camp_ out on the land. I'm gon-na try and get my—
Em
Ebm
___ soul free." We are
Chorus:
A7sus
Ab7sus
star - dust,_ we are___ gold -

Em
E♭m
D
D♭
en and we've got to get our - selves back to the
Em/B
E♭m/B♭
A7sus
A♭7sus
Em
E♭m
gar - den.
1.
2.
D.S. 𝄋 al Coda
2. Then
3. By the
Coda
flies a -

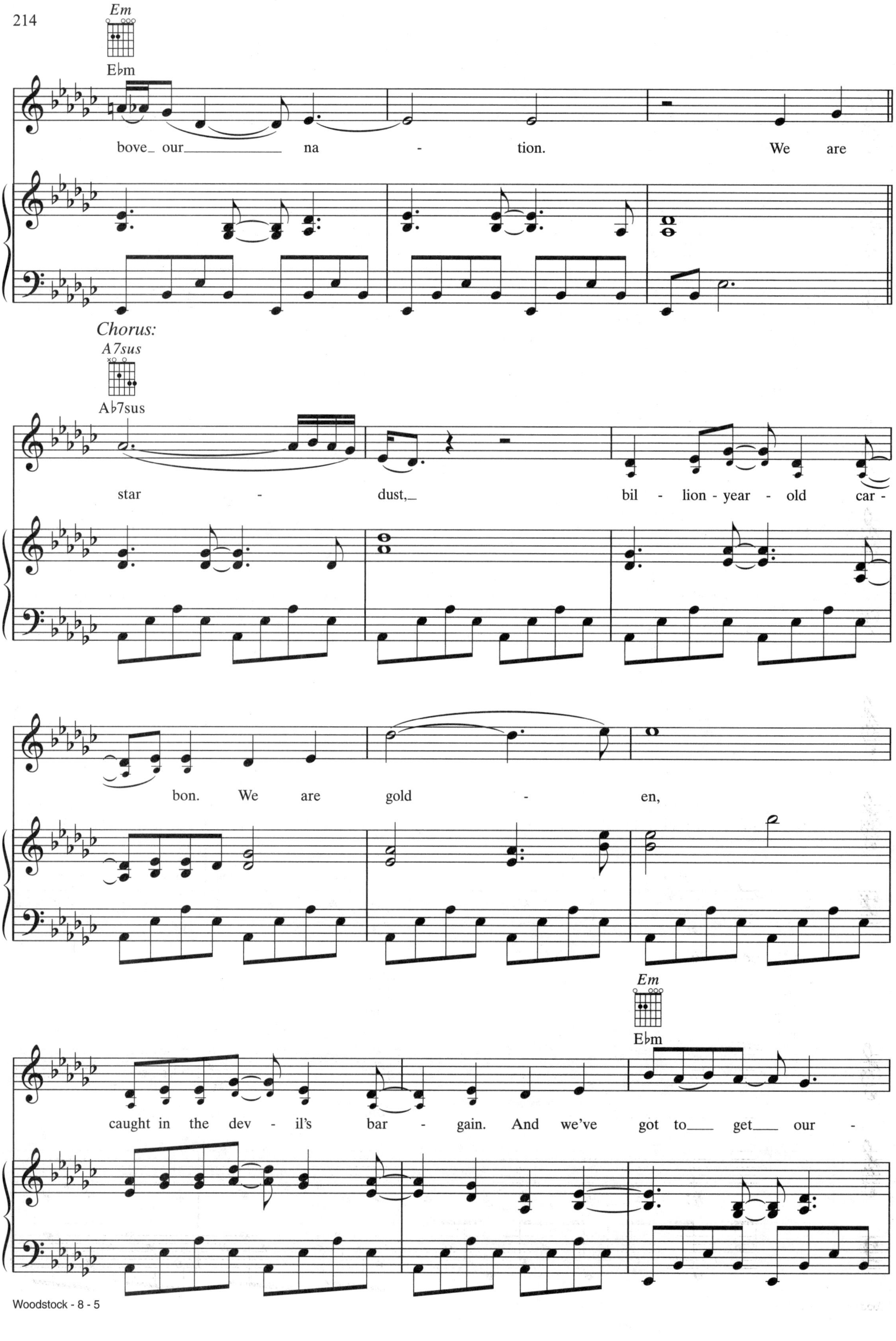
Em
E♭m
bove_ our_______ na - tion. We are
Chorus:
A7sus
A♭7sus
star - dust,_ bil - lion - year - old car -
bon. We are gold - en,
Em
E♭m
caught in the dev - il's bar - gain. And we've got to___ get___ our -

D
Em/B
G
D♭
E♭m/B♭
G♭
selves back to the gar -
Em
E♭m
den.
rit. poco a poco
Slower ♩ = 96
Em
E♭m
A7sus
A♭7sus
Oh, doo, doo, doo.

Em
Ebm
A7sus
Ab7sus
Oh, doo, doo, doo, doo,
Em/B
Ebm/Bb
A7sus
Ab7sus
doo, doo, doo, doo, doo, doo, doo, doo,
Em/B
Ebm/Bb
A7sus
Ab7sus
Em
Ebm
doo, doo, doo, doo, doo, doo, doo, doo, doo, doo.

Verse 2:
Then can I walk beside you?
I have come here to lose the smog
And I feel to be a cog in something turning
Maybe it is just the time of year
Or maybe it's the time of man
I don't know who I am
But you know life is for learning
(To Chorus:)

Verse 3:
By the time we got to Woodstock
We were half a million strong
And everywhere there was song and celebration
And I dreamed I saw the bombers
Riding shotgun in the sky and they were
Turning into butterflies above our nation
(To Coda)

YOU DON'T HAVE TO SAY YOU LOVE ME

English Lyrics by VICKI WICKHAM and SIMON NAPIER-BELL
Original Italian Lyrics by VITO PALLAVICINI

Music by
PINO DONAGGIO

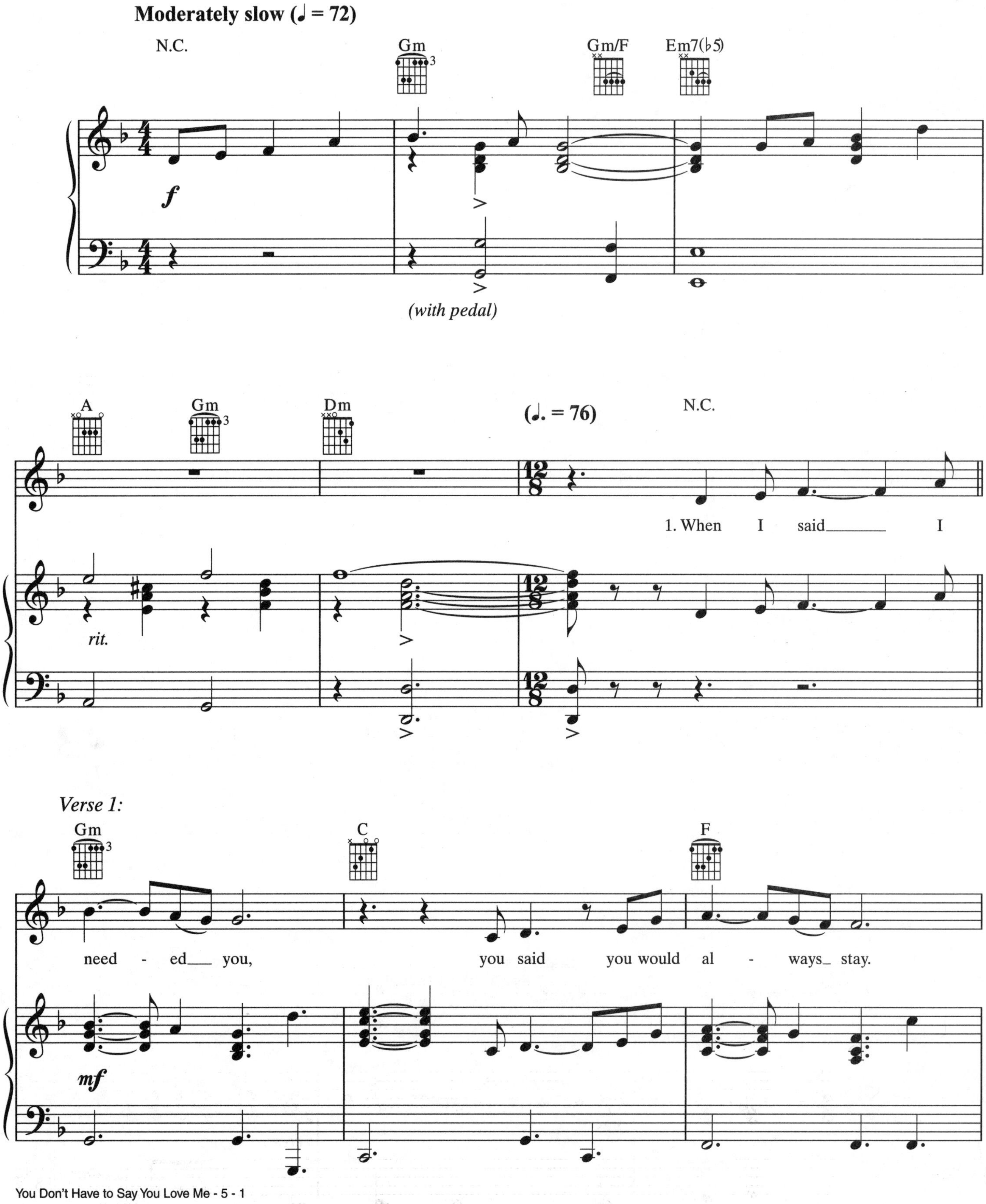

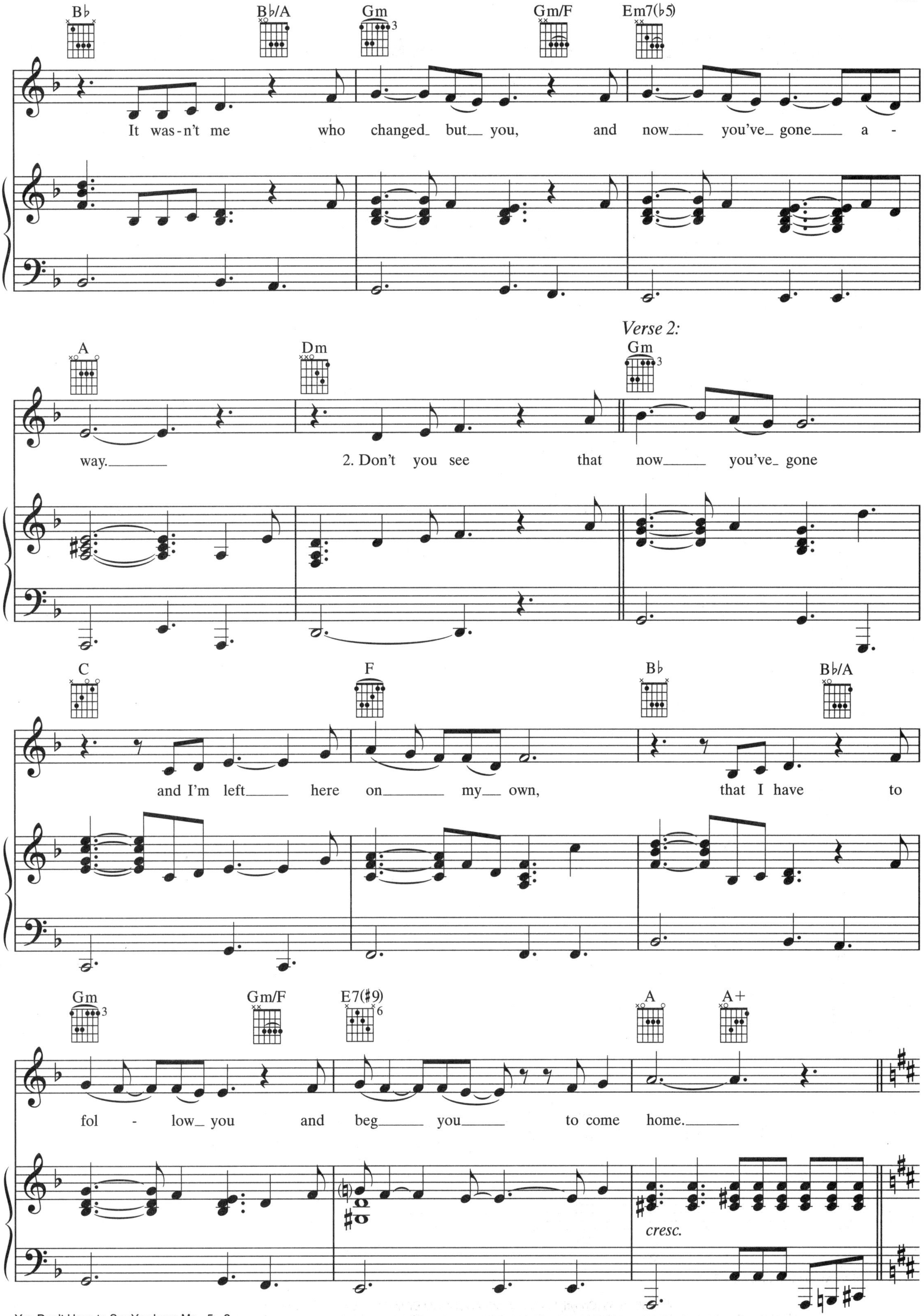
B♭
B♭/A
Gm
Gm/F
Em7(♭5)
It was-n't me who changed but you, and now you've gone a -
A
Dm
Verse 2:
Gm
way.
2. Don't you see that now you've gone
C
F
B♭
B♭/A
and I'm left here on my own, that I have to
Gm
Gm/F
E7(♯9)
A
A+
fol - low you and beg you to come home.
cresc.

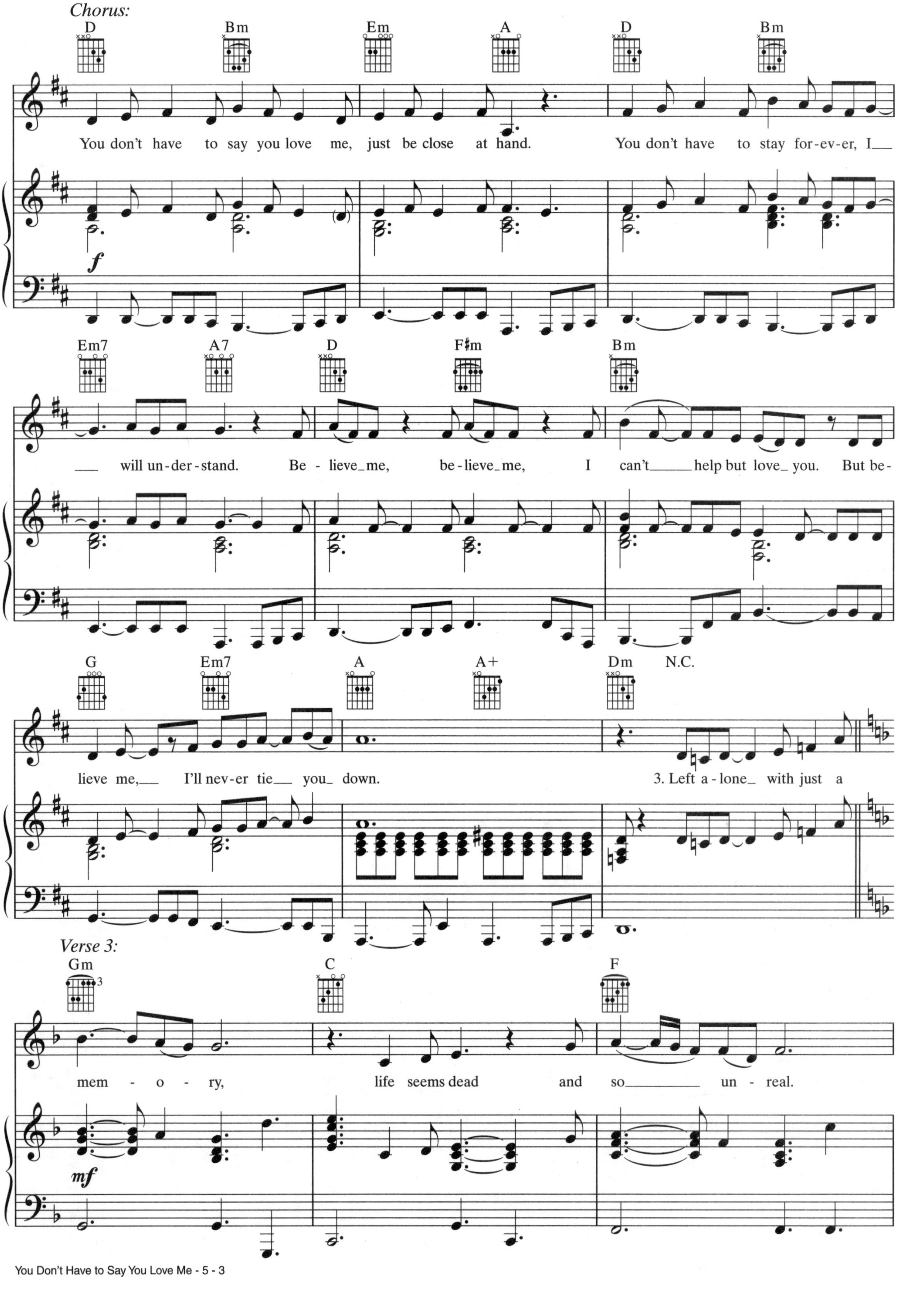
Chorus:
D Bm Em A D Bm
You don't have to say you love me, just be close at hand. You don't have to stay for-ev-er, I
f
Em7 A7 D F#m Bm
will un-der-stand. Be - lieve me, be-lieve me, I can't help but love you. But be-
G Em7 A A+ Dm N.C.
lieve me, I'll nev-er tie you down. 3. Left a-lone with just a
Verse 3:
Gm C F
mem - o - ry, life seems dead and so un - real.
mf

B♭ B♭/A Gm Gm/F A7
All that's left is lon - li - ness, there's noth-ing left to
Dm
feel.
Chorus:
D Bm Em A
You don't have to say you love me, just be close at hand.
D Bm Em7 A7 D
You don't have to stay for-ev-er, I will un-der-stand. Be - lieve me, be -

E
C♯m
F♯m
B
lieve me.
You don't have to say you love me, just be close at hand.
cresc.
f
E
C♯m
F♯m7
B7
E
D
You don't have to stay for-ev-er, I will un-der-stand. Be - lieve me, be -
E
D
E
lieve me, be - lieve me.

YOU ONLY LIVE TWICE

Music by JOHN BARRY
Lyric by LESLIE BRICUSSE

Moderately slow (♩ = 84)

*Original recording in B.

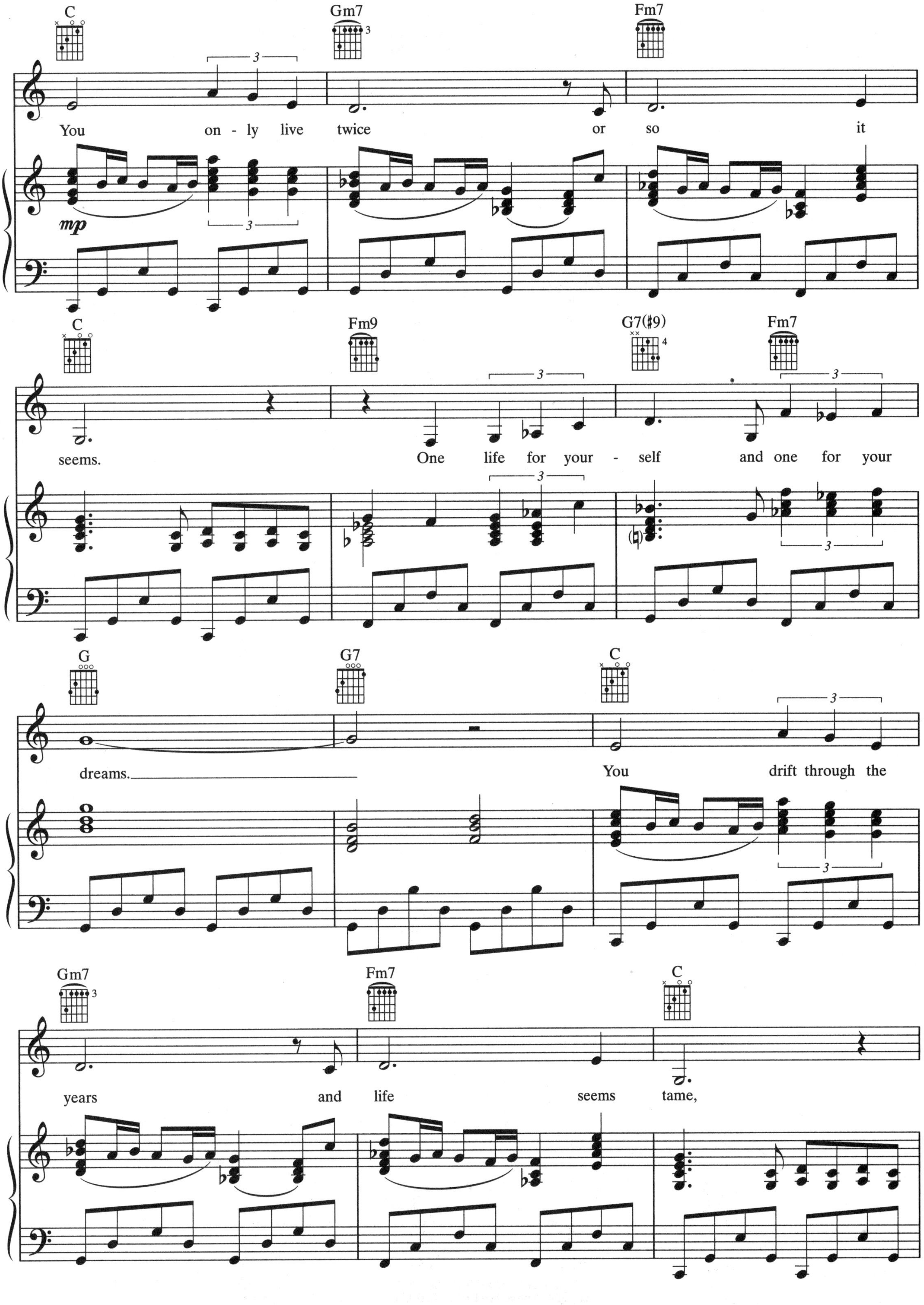
C
Gm7
Fm7
You on - ly live twice or so it
mp
C
Fm9
G7(♯9)
Fm7
seems. One life for your - self and one for your
G
G7
C
dreams. You drift through the
Gm7
Fm7
C
years and life seems tame,

Fm9
G7(♯9)
Fm7
C
till one dream ap - pears and love is it's name.
Fm7
G
And love is a strang - er
B♭m
G
Fm7
who'll beck - on you on.
Don't think of the
G
Fm7
G7
dan - ger or the strang - er is gone.

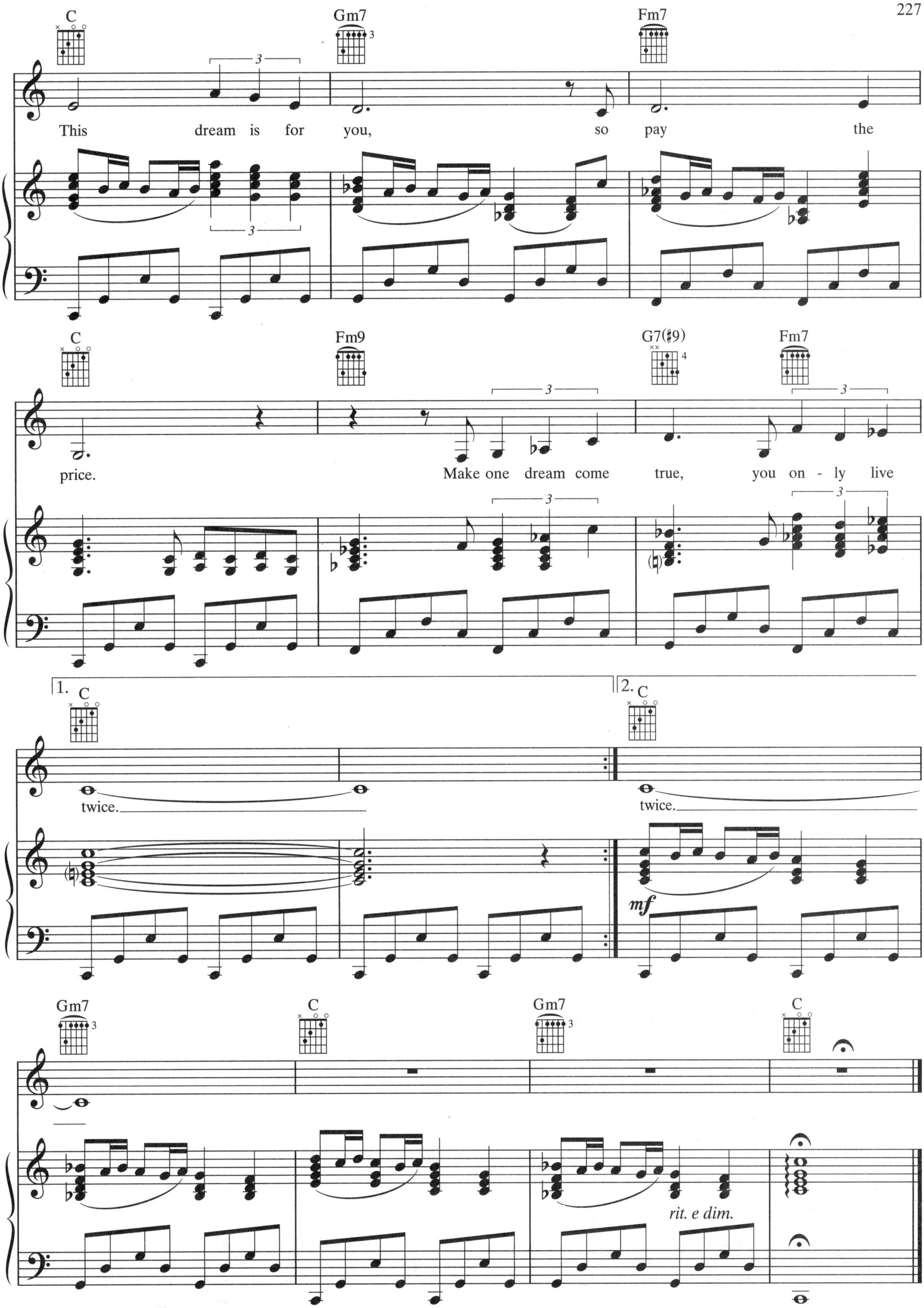
C
Gm7
Fm7
This dream is for you, so pay the
C
Fm9
G7(♯9)
Fm7
price. Make one dream come true, you on - ly live
1.
2.
twice.
twice.
mf
Gm7
C
Gm7
C
rit. e dim.

YOU SHOWED ME

Words and Music by
GENE CLARK and JIM McGUINN

A♭ B♭ A♭maj7
Oh, I love you.
We're in love we two.
Cm7 F7 Cm7 F7 Cm7 A♭ B♭
You showed me how to say, ex - act - ly what you say, in that ver - y spe - cial
La la la la la la la la la la la la la la la
Cm A♭ B♭ Cm
way. Oh, it's true.
la. Oh,
A♭ B♭ A♭maj7
To Coda
You fell for me too.
we're in love we two,

Bridge:
Ab Eb Fm Ab Eb
And when I tried it, I could see you
mf
Fm Ab Eb Fm
fall. And I de - cid - ed
F7 G7
D.S 𝄋 al Coda
it's not a trip at all.
𝄌 Coda
we're two.

Cm7 F7 Cm7 F7 Cm7 A♭ B♭
You showed me how to do ex - act - ly what you do, how I fell in love with
you.
You showed me how to say, ex - act - ly what you say in that ver - y spe - cial
way.
You taught it to me too, ex - act - ly what you do, and now you love me
Repeat and fade
too.__ Now you love me too.__ Now you love me
(Ah,__ ah.__) (Ah,__ ah.__)